THE
MAKER'S
DIET

DAILY REMINDERS

JORDAN S. RUBIN

SILOAM
A STRANG COMPANY

Most Strang Communications/Charisma House/Siloam/FrontLine/Realms products are available at special quantity discounts for bulk purchase for sales promotions, premiums, fund-raising, and educational needs. For details, write Strang Communications/Charisma House/Siloam/FrontLine/Realms, 600 Rinehart Road, Lake Mary, Florida 32746, or telephone (407) 333-0600.

The Maker's Diet Daily Reminders by Jordan S. Rubin
Published by Siloam
A Strang Company
600 Rinehart Road
Lake Mary, Florida 32746
www.siloam.com

Library of Congress Cataloging-in-Publication Data

Rubin, Jordan.
  The Maker's diet daily reminders / Jordan S. Rubin.
    p. cm.
  ISBN 1-59185-869-0 (casebound)
  1. Dieters--Prayer-books and devotions--English. 2. Nutrition--Religious aspects--Christianity--Meditations. 3. Food in the Bible--Meditations. 4. Rubin, Jordan. Maker's diet. I. Title.
BV4596.D53R83 2006
242'.4--dc22

2006019875

06 07 08 09 10 — 987654321
Printed in the United States of America

Introduction

Nearly twelve years ago I found myself suffering from an incurable illness. Its effective treatment escaped nearly seventy doctors. Yes, I felt hopeless. Yes, I was afraid. And yes, I felt deserted...but I wasn't alone. From the depths of my despair I heard a still, small voice say to me, "Everything is going to be OK."

After visiting what seemed like every doctor on the planet and trying every "miracle" drug, "miracle" diet, and "miracle" supplement, I found myself tearing through the pages of the world's oldest, most sacred, and best-selling book.

What I was looking for in the Bible was not purely spiritual. I was looking for answers to my many debilitating health problems. What I found was man's first health plan— and the only health program I will need for the rest of my life. This ancient health program literally transformed the life of a seemingly hopeless twenty-year-old, and since I first wrote about it, thousands of people have used these same principles to pull themselves out of the grip of disease and enter the promised land of health.

The health principles on which this program is based are essentially the same—yesterday, today, and forever. (See Hebrews 13:8.) You too can enjoy robust health and freedom from disease by simply following the health plan designed by our Creator.

The Maker's Diet is not merely a weight loss program...it is a lifestyle. *The Maker's Diet Daily Reminders* will help you sustain your commitment to the program by offering you daily encouragement and spiritual support. It presents life-changing health facts that are biblically based and scientifically proven, including a tip-a-day on boosting your immune system, attaining and maintaining your ideal weight, harnessing abundant energy, enhancing your physical appearance, reducing stress, improving digestion, and many more.

You owe it to yourself and everyone you care about to return to the Maker's Diet. This book will give you the support you need to do just that.

DAY 1

Many Americans assume that the United States is the world's healthiest nation. Unfortunately, statistics show that we are not as healthy as we might think.

We *do* enjoy one of the highest standards of living in the world, with extraordinary emergency medical technology and trauma care. But this fact doesn't make us *healthy*. When we learn what good health really means, and we begin to practice the good health habits God has set in place, we will experience the abundant life that He has for us.

> *The thief does not come except to steal, and to kill, and to destroy. I have come that they may have life, and that they may have it more abundantly.*
>
> —JOHN 10:10

Begin to pray that God's abundant life will be yours as you put the Maker's Diet into practice in your life.

DAY 2

Most people who end up in ambulances and emergency rooms get there because they had an accident or *a health crisis*. And the emergency care they receive is often life saving.

That is quite different from evaluating our national lifestyle to arrive at one of healthy living that *prevents* disease. The concept of preventative medicine has only recently been given media attention.

An ounce of prevention is worth a pound of cure.

—BENJAMIN FRANKLIN

Pray that God would give you the wisdom you need to *prevent* disease before it strikes.

DAY 3

Most Americans eat great quantities of food frequently, based on *convenience*. In fact, the entire fast-food and TV dinner industries have flourished due to our fast-paced lifestyles that demand we eat "convenient" foods.

Unfortunately, our Creator didn't design our bodies to operate at optimum levels on junk food, fast food, or prepackaged foods prepared in microwave ovens. His laws that govern our entire human nature, including our health, bring consequences when violated, whether or not we accept the fact that they are still in place. The good news is, however, that we can change our lifestyles and avoid the health problems so many others face.

Do you not know that your body is the temple of the Holy Spirit who is in you, whom you have from God, and you are not your own?

—1 CORINTHIANS 6:19

Begin to think of your body as the temple of God's Holy Spirit; good health and a long life will be the result.

DAY 4

Elmer A. Josephson, a pioneer who dared to challenge the stream of popular dietary trends, said, "There is no portion of the commandments of God in general, or of the Mosaic code in particular, that is not based on a scientific understanding of fundamental law. The laws of God are enforced and are as sure as the law of gravity."[1]

Oh, how I love Your law! It is my meditation all the day.

—PSALM 119:97

Make the commitment to memorize at least one verse of Scripture each week.

DAY 5

All of God's laws are like His law of gravity—*they can't be changed.* Our Creator specifically designed us to function best on the Maker's Diet. In order to benefit from His plan, we must examine exactly what food is "biblical" and what food is unclean, unhealthy, or unacceptable according to both God and science (in that order).

Jesus Christ is the same yesterday, today, and forever.

—HEBREWS 13:8

For one week, keep a food journal to see what foods you are consuming. You may be surprised at the amount of unhealthy food you actually eat.

DAY 6

Peter Rothschild, MD, PhD, wrote an unpublished book entitled *The Art of Health*. In a chapter called "Please Don't Eat the Wrapper," he writes:

> It suddenly dawned on us that God, the greatest master nutritionist of all times, has given us an all-purpose diet more than 3000 years ago.
>
> There is abundant historic evidence that reveals that the average Israelite, up to the end of the last century [19th], was much longer lived than the average Gentile.
>
> However, beginning with World War I, both diet and hygiene began to slacken among the children of Israel all over the planet, until only a small fraction remains true to biblical tradition.... The trend of longevity is gradually vanishing among the non-observant. It appears that God indeed knew what nourishment to recommend.[2]

> *He sent His word and healed them, and delivered them from their destructions.*
>
> —PSALM 107:20

For a high-energy snack, slice a large date in half, remove the pit, insert a raw pecan into each half, and then sprinkle with coconut flakes. It's the perfect snack to stave off junk-food cravings.

DAY 7

Michael D. Jacobson, DO, has noted that in the mid-fourteenth century, bubonic plague wiped out one-fourth of Europe's population in just one year. But read history's record of how the Jewish people fared in the face of it:

Hundreds of years prior to the discovery of bacteria, the Jews were protecting themselves from the deadly *Yersinia pestis* microbe by practicing cleanliness and good hygiene....More than three thousand years before man discovered bacteria, the Creator had given detailed instructions that, if followed, would prevent the spread of such a deadly communicable disease.[3]

He who has clean hands and a pure heart...shall receive blessing from the Lord.

—Psalm 24:4–5

If you are planning to travel to a foreign country, be sure to pack an organic hand sanitizer and use it frequently.

DAY 8

In his book *Nutrition and Physical Degeneration,* Dr. Weston A. Price concluded that diet was the only possible factor accounting for universal good physical health among primitive people. People who ate the modern diet suffered from physical degeneration, while those on primitive diets did not. He suggested that dietary deficiencies also contributed to poor brain development and associated social disorders such as juvenile delinquency and high crime rates.

Price dared to suggest that modern humans learn from primitives (in an era when it was fashionable to disparage and sneer at primitive people groups), and he strongly urged a return to the primitive diet that made our ancestors so healthy.

I have seen his ways, and will heal him; I will

> *also lead him, and restore comforts to him and*
> *to his mourners.*
> —Isaiah 57:18

Dental health is a good indication of physical health. Be sure to schedule teeth cleanings and dental checkups every six months.

DAY 9

According to scriptures common to the Judeo-Christian tradition, the "bowels," or the "belly," are described as the seat of the emotions. Surprisingly, the English word *gut* reflects a highly accurate view of the intestinal tract. One dictionary defines *gut* as "the basic visceral or emotional part of a person…the alimentary canal or part of it (as the intestine or stomach)…[and] the inner essential parts."[4] The gut is an extremely important part of your body—perhaps as important as your brain—since it is where many of your emotions are experienced.

> *My beloved put in his hand by the hole of the*
> *door, and my bowels were moved for him.*
> —Song of Solomon 5:4, kjv

Eating several small meals rather than two or three large ones keeps your sugar level stable and prevents mood swings and headaches—and helps you maintain a stable energy level throughout the day.

DAY 10

Digestive complaints result in more time lost at work, school, and play than any other health-related problem.[5] Interestingly enough, according to epidemiological research, many of these digestive problems were rare or nonexistent less than a century ago!

What did our ancestors know or do that we do not? How can we reclaim the health enjoyed by the ancients? For one thing, they ate a diet similar to the Maker's Diet and maintained physically vigorous lifestyles.

Food sustains us, it can be a source of considerable pleasure…it adds valued dimension to our lives. Yet what we eat may affect our risk for several of the leading causes of death for Americans.[6]
—Dr. C. Everett Koop, Former Surgeon General of the United States

Flaxseed oil—the "feel-good" fat—is high in omega-3 fatty acids, which help fight fatigue, dry skin, itchy scalp, dandruff, arthritis pain, allergies, and constipation, while improving eyesight and color perception. Consume 2 tablespoons daily.

DAY 11

In the nineteenth century, hundreds of thousands of European women were dying of childbirth fever until a Viennese obstetrician named Dr. Semmelweis rediscovered biblical hygiene. Dr. Semmelweis went against the grain of established medical practice and asked every doctor and medical student to wash their hands between deliveries (and autopsies). When they did, the death rate dropped by 90 percent![7]

[The priest] shall take off his garments, put on

> *other garments, and carry the ashes outside the*
> *camp to a clean place.*
>
> —LEVITICUS 6:11

Not only is washing your hands a good idea to combat germs, but when you are finished, invigorate your senses by splashing cold water on your face and running your hands and wrists under the cold water tap.

DAY 12

The allergy industry treats allergies through the exclusive use of drugs that either desensitize the immune system toward potential allergens or suppress its natural response system altogether. Most of these drugs have multiple side effects and are only marginally effective. While we can't ignore the suffering, we can take a simpler, commonsense approach to the problem.

The concepts of advanced hygiene offer better cleansing techniques that will keep most of the offending substances away from your body (and may even avoid triggering an immune system response altogether).

> *O LORD my God, I cried out to You, and You*
> *healed me.*
>
> —PSALM 30:2

Reduce the amount of allergens you come in contact with by washing bed linens and drapes frequently and preventing pets with fur dander from entering the bedroom.

DAY 13

Long before the factories of the Industrial Age and the existence of modern grocery stores, people tended to get dirty just gathering or harvesting their food. The longest-lived people were exposed to all sorts of microscopic bugs living in the soil. Life in the pre–Industrial Age depended on what grew and lived in and on the earth. "Dirt" and "soil" were not negative concepts in the minds of our primitive ancestors.

> *You visit the earth and water it, You greatly enrich it; the river of God is full of water; You provide their grain, for so You have prepared it.*
> —Psalm 65:9

Eat as many non-processed foods as you can—foods that are as close to their natural environment as possible.

DAY 14

Water supplies from wells and rivers once teemed with mycobacteria, including some pathogens that were downright deadly. Chlorine and other disinfectant substances helped make our public water supplies much safer than a century ago, and that is important to the public health. Unfortunately, most public water purification systems neglect to *remove* the chlorine after it has done its job in the water. For this reason, it is important to purify your own water as much as possible.

> *[The man who fears the Lord] shall be like a tree planted by the rivers of water, that brings forth its fruit in its season, whose leaf also shall not wither; and whatever he does shall prosper.*
> —Psalm 1:3

At the very least, filter your tap water with a high-quality purification system to remove the chlorine.

DAY 15

Yeast and fungal organisms are especially aggressive in weakened intestinal systems. When antibiotics kill the harmful bacteria they are targeting, they also indiscriminately decimate the friendly bacteria in the body. This allows other harmful bacteria, yeast, and fungi in the body, which are normally held in check by the friendly bacteria, to begin to multiply profusely, causing other disease conditions.

> *To be or not to be is not the question. The question is how to prolong being.*
> —TOM ROBBINS, AMERICAN NOVELIST

Be sure to eat plenty of yogurt or cottage cheese after you finish any round of antibiotics.

DAY 16

Anyone with intractable autoimmune conditions, allergies, low energy, inability to gain weight, fibromyalgia, and chronic fatigue syndrome should take advantage of SBOs (soil-based organisms). The newly recognized ability of soil organisms to aid our quest for healing and maintaining good health is one of the most exciting breakthroughs in modern health. And isn't it ironic that we are talking about soil organisms as old as the earth itself?

The people who live long are those who love to live.

—Anonymous

If you or your children constantly battle chronic middle-ear infections, beginning SBO supplementation will increase your resistance and decrease the likelihood of a recurrence.

DAY 17

Dr. Joseph Mercola believes the timing of your sleep affects its quality. He says, "The more hours that you can sleep before midnight, the better off you will be."[8] He cites a study published in the *Lancet* (a respected medical journal in Great Britain) indicating that chronic sleep loss produces serious symptoms mimicking the effects of aging and the early stages of diabetes.[9] And finally, according to the late Elmer Josephson, "Authorities tell us that one hour of sleep before midnight is equivalent to four hours afterward."[10]

Early to bed, early to rise, makes a man happy, healthy, and wise.

—Benjamin Franklin

Choose a bedtime that works for you, preferably before midnight, and stick to it—both on weekdays and on weekends.

DAY 18

How to get sick recommendation #1: Stay out of the sun. Civilizations throughout history have understood that the sun is vital to human health. The human skin uses the energy from the sun to manufacture vitamin D for the body. This hormone/vitamin is important for many reasons, including its role in strengthening immune system function and proper mineral absorption.

I think you might dispense with half your doctors if you would only consult Dr. Sun more.
—HENRY WARD BEECHER, PROTESTANT
CLERGYMAN AND REFORMER

Spend a reasonable amount of time in the sunshine each day; it will improve your mood—and your health!

DAY 19

How to get sick recommendation #2: Go to bed after midnight. This is a great way to get sick. From biblical times to just before the Industrial Revolution, people used to go to sleep and rise with the setting and rising of the sun. This is the natural way to link your peak activity to the body's natural hormonal rhythms.

Sleep is the best-kept beauty and energy secret around.
—ANONYMOUS

Before you go to bed, make a list of all the tasks and worries that you are to face the next day. Write them all out, and then leave them there. Don't take them with you to bed.

DAY 20

How to get sick recommendation #3: Never let them see you sweat. Any attempt to artificially prevent perspiration is very unhealthy because perspiration is the Maker's method of safely cooling the body while excreting numerous toxins. Suppressing this natural sweat response in your underarms or other areas blocks the body's cleansing process and the natural flow of the lymphatic system.

> *Health of body and mind is a great blessing.*
> —JOHN HENRY CARDINAL NEWMAN, VICAR OF
> SAINT MARY'S, OXFORD, ENGLAND

Select an underarm *deodorant* rather than an *antiperspirant* to use under your arms.

DAY 21

How to get sick recommendation #4: Take megavitamins. The use of massive amounts of vitamins and minerals is very unnatural—especially the popular and cheap synthetic and isolated "vitamins" created in chemical plants and widely sold in discount retail stores. The human body was not designed to consume such artificial products, especially in such excessive amounts. Nature prevents us from consuming 20,000 mg of vitamin C in one day because it is impossible to consume three hundred oranges (a natural source of vitamin C) in one day!

> *Half the modern drugs could well be thrown out the window, except that the birds might eat them.*
> —MARTIN H. FISCHER, AUTOMOBILE DESIGNER

When looking for a brand of vitamin to use, choose "living food supplements" over the cheaper synthetic type.

DAY 22

*H*ow to get sick recommendation #5: Use fluoride toothpaste *and mouthwash, and drink fluoridated water.* Fluoride is extremely poisonous—especially the salt-based form used in toothpaste and mouthwash. In addition, its true effectiveness in preventing tooth decay is questionable at best.

> *The LORD will guide you continually, and satisfy your soul in drought, and strengthen your bones; you shall be like a watered garden, and like a spring of water, whose waters do not fail.*
> —ISAIAH 58:11

Choose nonfluoridated alternatives in toothpaste and mouthwash for your oral hygiene needs.

DAY 23

*H*ow to get sick recommendation #6: Use artificial sweet*eners and avoid sugars.* As bad as sugar can be in its various forms, artificial sweeteners are worse! Some are downright deadly because of their carcinogenic properties and their use in such high-volume products as diet soft drinks and sugar-free foods. If the Maker didn't produce it "as is," then it probably isn't much better than the other synthetic sugar substitutes.

> *Our prayer should be for a sound mind and a healthy body.*
> —JUVENAL, ROMAN PHILOSOPHER AND SATIRIST

Choose unrefined, natural sugar products rather than artificial sweeteners.

DAY 24

*H*ow to get sick recommendation #7: Shower every day, but *don't take a bath.* Excessive showering—even in the purest water—can actually rob your hair and body of its natural oils.[11] It can also alter your body's pH level (especially if you're using certain alkaline shampoos and soaps). If the Maker has a preference, it might be the use of ritual bathing that combined bathing (washing in a shallow bath) with sprinkling (showering for brief periods of time).

> *I have good health, good thoughts, and good humor, thanks be to God Almighty.*
> —WILLIAM BYRD, ENGLISH COMPOSER

Try to include a combination of bathing and showering in your personal hygiene routine.

DAY 25

*H*ow to get sick recommendation #8: Swim in chlorinated pools, *and drink and shower with chlorinated water.* Chlorine is an effective bacteria killer, although some strains of bacteria are developing a resistance to chlorine. Unfortunately, chlorine is an indiscriminate killer that kills both friendly and unfriendly bacteria. It also eats through lead pipes, corrodes most metals, and harms cells and DNA strands in virtually every living thing it touches. Chlorine also introduces to our water supplies some highly carcinogenic chemicals.

> *A sound mind in a sound body is a short but full description of a happy state in this world.*
> —JOHN LOCKE, SEVENTEENTH-CENTURY
> ENGLISH PHILOSOPHER

If you own a swimming pool, use nonchlorinated alternatives to maintain the cleanliness of the pool.

DAY 26

*H*ow to get sick recommendation #9: Don't breast-feed your *baby.* Breast-feeding helps babies avoid the trauma of numerous childhood diseases—and unnecessary hospital bills. It also reduces the mother's risk of developing breast cancer by 25 percent, and it may even lower the risk of postpartum depression! Mother's milk contains cells that attack harmful bacteria in the baby's system, and it is able to form antibodies that destroy invading viruses as well.[12]

> *It's bizarre that the produce manager is more important to my children's health than the pediatrician.*
>
> —MERYL STREEP, ACTRESS

Mother's milk is the Maker's perfect food for babies, delivered in the close bonds of maternal intimacy.

DAY 27

*H*ow to get sick recommendation #10: Get tattoos. The Scriptures warn against piercing the skin. Body piercing and tattoos can easily introduce potentially deadly infections and toxic foreign substances into the body and bloodstream. Some health providers warn that even tiny puncture wounds might block important electrical nerve impulses just under the skin.

> *You shall not make any cuttings in your flesh ... nor tattoo any marks on you: I am the LORD.*
>
> —LEVITICUS 19:28

If you already have a tattoo, there is no medical reason for you to have it removed; however, if you value your health, do not consent to any further tattoos.

DAY 28

How to get sick recommendation #11: Get all of your immunization shots. Despite massive media and government public relations campaigns to the contrary, certain childhood immunization injections may pose considerable risks to children. Most adults today received one to five immunizations in childhood, but schoolchildren today receive an average of twenty-two or more immunizations—most of them administered while the brain and nervous system are still developing!

> *Health is worth more than learning.*
>
> —THOMAS JEFFERSON

Most states allow philosophical and religious exemptions from mandatory immunization programs should you decide this is the way to go.

DAY 29

How to get sick recommendation #12: Travel in airplanes often. Some people who spend a lot of time at high altitudes experience problems with infertility and oxygen production in the body. The body adapts well to high altitudes for short periods of time, but not for long periods. Some researchers believe that the atmospheric pressures and radiation to which airplane travelers are exposed are the equivalent of hundreds of CAT scans and pose the greatest oxidative stress on the human body.[13] Besides, who wants to be trapped in a small room with hundreds of sneezing, coughing people?

Health is not valued until sickness comes.
—DR. THOMAS FULLER, BRITISH PHYSICIAN

While it is difficult to avoid airplane travel altogether, try to travel by car, train, or some other means of transportation as frequently as you can.

DAY 30

How to get sick recommendation #13: Expose yourself often to electromagnetic energy. Everywhere you go, you run into electromagnetic fields (EMFs) from television sets, microwave ovens, cell phones, and local media transmission towers. Hospital body scans (X-rays and their computerized cousin, computerized axial tomography [CAT scans]) and magnetic resonance imaging (MRI) expose us to especially high levels of EMFs. Cellular phones may also pose dangers to brain tissues due to the close proximity of delicate brain tissue to the powerful EMF transmitters.

Happiness is nothing more than good health and a bad memory.

—ALBERT SCHWEITZER

Avoid getting too close to or spending too much near the following objects when they are in use: hair dryers, microwave ovens, television sets, computers, and cell phones.

DAY 31

How to get sick recommendation #14: *Use a lot of skin care products, cosmetics, hair care products, nail care products, shampoos, soaps, perfumes, shaving cream, suntan lotion, and antibacterial soaps.* Beware of skin care or other types of cosmetic products that cause harm by destroying the skin's or hair's natural pH and by introducing potentially dangerous toxins into your body.

Health is not simply the absence of sickness.
—HANNAH GREEN, AMERICAN NOVELIST

Plenty of regular soap, sufficiently heated running water, and thorough scrubbing will do the job just as well with no side effects.

DAY 32

How to get sick recommendation #15: *Take lots of medications.* Every medicine has a side effect. There may be a time and place for the use of medication, but much of the prescription activity in the U.S. perpetuates health problems by treating symptoms rather than their root causes.

A wise man should consider that health is the greatest of human blessings, and learn how by his own thought to derive benefit from his illness.
—HIPPOCRATES

You can get similar health benefits with no side effects by consuming foods such as cold-water fish, fruits and vegetables high in antioxidants, and certain botanicals that naturally reduce the Cox-2 enzyme and provide other anti-inflammatory benefits.[14]

DAY 33

How to get sick recommendation #16: Get your cavities filled with mercury. For more than 150 years, the dental profession has carefully avoided using the term *mercury* when describing the material used to fill tooth cavities for millions of Americans. Instead they called it "silver amalgam," "silver fillings," or "amalgam fillings." The true composition of dental amalgam is 45 to 55 percent mercury, with about 30 percent silver and other metals such as copper, tin, and zinc. Unfortunately, mercury is a heavy metal toxin and is more detrimental to your body than it is beneficial to your teeth.

As I see it, every day you do one of two things: build health or produce disease within yourself.
—ADELLE DAVIS, NUTRITIONIST

It may be difficult to find a dentist in your area who will fill your cavities with more natural materials, but it isn't impossible, and the benefits are worth it.

DAY 34

How to get sick recommendation #17: Do aerobic exercise. While I believe strongly in the need for regular exercise, my research indicates that high-intensity aerobic exercise producing a very high elevated heart rate for long periods of time through vigorous exercise such as jogging or running on hard surfaces is essentially unnatural to the body.

&

*An early morning walk is a blessing for the whole
day.*

—HENRY DAVID THOREAU

Take a brisk, vigorous fifteen- to twenty-minute walk twice each
day.

DAY 35

H*ow to get sick recommendation #18: Wear contact lenses
and receive implants of other foreign objects, such as silicone breast implants.* Media reports constantly feature hor-
ror stories of movie stars (and ordinary people) whose lives
were ruined after receiving silicone implants that burst,
hardened within their bodies, or inflamed nearby tissues.
Even contact lenses, especially the soft lens variety offered
for long-term wear, pose significant infection risks to the
wearers under certain conditions.

These products offer certain conveniences and
cosmetic benefits, but remember that they are still foreign
objects that the Maker never intended for us to insert into
the human body.[15]

&

*Keeping your body healthy is an expression of
gratitude to the Creator.*

—THICH HANH, VIETNAMESE TEACHER AND POET

Whenever possible, wear glasses rather than contact lenses.

DAY 36

H*ow to get sick recommendation #19: Live in a toxic home
with toxic paint, carpet, mold, paraffin candles, etc.* You

could fill a small library with the books and official research reports written on this subject. Do some research if you or your family suffers from allergies or unexplained physical symptoms. Many popular building materials, including plywood, particle board, treated lumber, adhesives, paint, paint thinners, insulation, paint strippers, carpets, carpet pads—and even decorative paraffin candles—contain highly toxic materials. These can enter your living area as gaseous vapors and increase the toxic load on the body.

The more severe the problem, pain, or illness, the more severe will be the necessary changes. These may involve breaking bad habits, making changes in life, or acquiring new and better ways of living.

—PETER MCWILLIAMS, AMERICAN AUTHOR

Research the areas or products used in your home that might be causing toxicity, and then develop a plan to remove them from your home environment.

DAY 37

How to get sick recommendation #20: *Wear synthetic fabrics.* The Maker's natural fibers produce the ideal clothing for the human body. Such natural fibers as wool and cotton are far better for the human body because they "breathe" and are better suited to handling human perspiration while preserving balanced body temperatures in hot or cold climates.

Look to your health; if you have it, praise God and value it next to conscience; for health is the

> *second blessing that we mortals are capable of, a*
> *blessing money can't buy.*
> —Izaak Walton, Author

Whenever possible, choose cotton blends of fabric for your clothing, rather than polyester or any other synthetic material.

DAY 38

How to get sick recommendation #21: Breathe with shallow breaths. The Maker gave you two lungs with an amazing air capacity. Unfortunately, most of us use only a fraction of our lung capacity, and we suffer for it. Not only should people avoid cigarettes or air pollution to keep from breathing in toxins, but they also should breathe more deeply the life-giving oxygen that God has placed in our atmosphere.

❧

> *The only way for a rich man to be healthy is, by*
> *exercise and abstinence, to live as if he were poor.*
> —Sir William Temple, British Diplomat,
> Essayist

Proper breathing involves breathing from the abdomen or "belly" instead of from the chest. If your stomach moves outward when you take a deep breath, then you have learned the secret of breathing fully from the diaphragm.

DAY 39

How to get sick recommendation #22: Swallow your food without chewing well (or at all). Chewing is extremely important to proper digestion. The ultimate goal of the process is to deliver food to the stomach in a liquid state. I recommend chewing each bite twenty-five to fifty times as needed—especially when eating foods high in carbohydrates, such as grains, sugars, and starches.

❧

Sharing food with another human being is an intimate act that should not be indulged in lightly.
—M. F. K. FISHER, AMERICAN AUTHOR

Always eat sitting down, and avoid watching TV, arguing, or doing something else that requires concentration while you are eating.

DAY 40

How to get sick recommendation #23: Use plastic food storage products and the popular food wraps, and reuse plastic drinking bottles.** Plastic products release or leach carcinogenic toxins into foods. The toxicity is increased when foods contain high amounts of water or when they are highly acidic. Water is one of nature's most effective solvents, and it is effective at drawing out toxins from plastic.

❧

So many people spend their health gaining wealth, and then have to spend their wealth to regain their health.
—A. J. REB MATERI, HEALTH WRITER

Do not use plastic water bottles more than twice at the most.

DAY 41

How to get sick recommendation #24: Eat grocery store produce and processed foods treated with pesticides, herbicides, animal growth hormones, and antibiotics; don't forget hybridized, irradiated, and genetically altered foods.** What a mouthful—literally! Pesticides and herbicides comprise one of the world's most deadly classes of chemical compounds. If a pesticide or herbicide kills one thing, it will probably kill, mutate, or seriously damage a whole host of other things. The problem with these compounds is that they tend to stay on the fruit, vegetable, or plant they were applied to.

> *You don't have to cook fancy or complicated masterpieces—just good food from fresh ingredients.*
>
> —JULIA CHILD

Be sure to wash any store-bought fruits and vegetables you may purchase.

DAY 42

How to get sick recommendation #25: *Wear tight underclothing.* The body's lymph system is absolutely crucial to the immune system. It is the first line of defense against cancer cells, toxins, and viral and bacterial attacks. Lymph nodes that are compressed or blocked by tight clothing may not allow the lymph system to be properly cleansed.

> *The only way to keep your health is to eat what you don't want, drink what you don't like, and do what you'd druther not.*
>
> —MARK TWAIN

Women should not wear bras to bed.

DAY 43

How to get sick recommendation #26: *Undergo surgery to remove "unnecessary body parts."* You take your life into your hands every time you agree to enter a hospital for surgery. And your tonsils and appendix are not unnecessary, as some doctors may say. If it was there when you were born, chances are your Maker intended for it to stay there until you die!

It is better to lose health like a spendthrift than to waste it like a miser.
—ROBERT LOUIS STEVENSON

Never undergo a tonsillectomy or appendectomy as a preventive measure—only elect these procedures if they are medically necessary.

DAY 44

How to get sick recommendation #27: Visit your medical doctor often. While I am thankful for all of the wonderful medical breakthroughs and excellent emergency medical care available in this country, you might want to know that, according to the *Journal of the American Medical Association*, doctors are the third leading cause of death in the U.S., causing 250,000 deaths every year.[16] Most doctors are sincere, hard-working professionals who try to do their jobs well. However, the American health-care system as a whole leaves a lot to be desired.

Joy and Temperance and Repose,
Slam the door on the doctor's nose.
—HENRY WADSWORTH LONGFELLOW

Do not run to your family physician every time a minor illness arises; instead, try to treat the problem in a more natural way.

DAY 45

In most cases, the things you do and say begin with the things you *think* and *believe*. You are barraged by stressing circumstances and challenges every day. How do you deal with them? (Or do you even try?)

Imagine your life as a glass filled to the halfway mark with water. How would you describe your "life"? Is your glass "half full" or "half empty"? Your answer may reveal a lot about your thought life and life view. A positive view would say "half full," considering what you have; a negative view would say "half empty," focusing on what you don't have.

For whatever is in your heart determines what you say. A good person produces good words from a good heart, and an evil person produces evil words from an evil heart.
—MATTHEW 12:34–35, NLT

Fill your mind with God's Word, and you will begin to act out what you put in.

DAY 46

Stress is a natural part of life. Some experts say that stress *is* life. Psychologist and author Dr. Kevin Lehman said the best definition for stress he has ever found was, "The wear and tear on our bodies produced by the very process of living."[17] He explained that stress comes from good things as well as bad circumstances, but trouble comes when it goes on for days and weeks.

It reminds me of buying the best DieHard battery

you can find, but if you have a habit of leaving the lights on, even a DieHard finally runs down.
—DR. KEVIN LEHMAN, CHRISTIAN PSYCHOLOGIST
AND BEST-SELLING AUTHOR

Stop and take a "relaxation break" during the most stressful part of your day.

DAY 47

Biblical prayer incorporates more than words—it often includes the healing touch of caring people of faith, and the results are often nothing less than miraculous. In the very least, they are comforting in times of need.

🐟

Is anyone among you sick? Let him call for the elders of the church, and let them pray over him, anointing him with oil in the name of the Lord.
—JAMES 5:14

Allow others to build you up and pray for you—it is an important part of the healing process.

DAY 48

Dr. Don Colbert has noted that research conducted by the Department of Behavioral Medicine at the UCLA Medical School into the physical benefits of happiness proved conclusively that "laughter, happiness and joy are perfect antidotes for stress." Colbert added, "A noted doctor once said that the diaphragm, thorax, abdomen, heart, lungs—and even the liver—are given a massage during a hearty laugh."[18]

A merry heart does good, like medicine.

—Proverbs 17:22

Rent a comedy classic or watch old reruns of *I Love Lucy* or *The Three Stooges*, and reap the healthy benefits of laughter.

DAY 49

We have a world to explore and master, and we can't do it if our bodies are accumulating fat and our muscles, joints, and internal organs are breaking down. We all need exercise.

From my research, I am convinced that the Creator's prescription for exercise more closely resembles real-life activities involved in the daily patterns of work and play. This is in sharp contrast to the high-impact aerobic exercises that many people do today.

Too many people confine their exercise to jumping to conclusions, running up bills, stretching the truth, bending over backward, lying down on the job, sidestepping responsibility, and pushing their luck.

—Anonymous

We *do* need exercise for maximum health, but high-stress aerobic exercise does not deliver as promised and can cause more harm than good.

DAY 50

Here is a quick course on deep breathing just to get you started:

1. Sit or lie down and relax.
2. Place a hand on your abdomen to see if it expands as you breathe. If only your chest moves with your breaths, you are "shallow breathing."
3. Breathe deeply through your mouth, and breathe "all the way down to your belly button." Your abdomen (stomach), not your chest, should rise as you inhale.
4. Hold your breath for a few seconds, and then exhale slowly and fully.[19]

Be still, and know that I am God.

—Psalm 46:10

With more practice, you will revert back to the instinctive deep-breathing way you began life.

DAY 51

Medicinal herbalist James A. Duke, PhD, former chief of the USDA Medicinal Plant Laboratory and author of *Herbs of the Bible: 2000 Years of Plant Medicine*, states, "The Bible mentions 128 plants that were part of the everyday life of ancient Israel and of its Mediterranean neighbors."[20]

Don't wait for the "right moment" to begin to live healthier. That moment may never come.
—Stephanie Tourles, Self-help Author

To "charge up" your mental capsule, try ginkgo biloba. This popular supplement boosts circulation to the brain, enhancing memory and alertness.

DAY 52

The Bible often mentions the names of herbs, although it rarely goes into great detail about the use of healing herbs. However, herbs were so highly valued in biblical times that the desire for herb or "vegetable" gardens spawned murder plots and national atrocities.

King Ahab's wife, the infamous Jezebel, took matters into her own lethal hands when Naboth refused to sell his vineyard. (The New International and New American versions translates it "vegetable garden.") Jezebel had Naboth stoned to death so that King Ahab could have the garden he always wanted. (See 1 Kings 21:2–13.)

May yours endure a long and fruitful season.
—JULIE PERKINS CANTRELL, AUTHOR

Drink green tea instead of a black tea whenever possible. This earthy, natural energizer is rich in antioxidants and has only one-fifth the caffeine of black tea, so it won't make you jittery or stain your teeth.

DAY 53

Myrrh was a cure-all treatment in Mesopotamia, Greece, and the Roman Empire. Myrrh used in a mouthwash can stop infections, and the herb is an effective treatment for bronchial and vaginal infections.[21] Myrrh contains a compound called furanosesquiterpenoid, which deactivates a protein in cancer cells that resists chemotherapy, according to researchers at Rutgers University.[22]

To accept the responsibility of being a child of

> *God is to accept the best that life has to offer you.*
> —STELLA TERRILL MANN, WRITER

Take myrrh as a preventative against leukemia, breast cancer, and cancers of the prostate, ovaries, and lungs.

DAY 54

A great way to use essential oils is to put five to ten drops into a warm bath. That is a true healing treat. You can also rub a few drops of these oils into the soles of your feet. You can even gain benefit from inhaling directly from the bottle. If you have small children, try applying essential oils to their stuffed animals or to the inside of their pillowcase each night.

> *After a tiring day, soothe those tight muscles by filling the bathtub with either an essential oil or two cups of Epsom salts and hot water (stimulating but not scalding). Sink into the tub and lounge with a towel or bath pillow behind your head. When the water begins to cool, stand up and turn on the shower. Rinse off with a blast of cold water, then end with a warming stream.*
> —BARBARA L. HELLER, PSYCHOTHERAPIST AND
> AUTHOR

Several times a week bathe in warm water that has five to ten drops of an essential oil.

DAY 55

History reveals that the healthiest people in the world were generally the most *primitive* people as well! Our ancestors rarely died from the diet- and lifestyle-related illnesses that kill most modern people before their time, mainly because they ate more healthfully and had more active lifestyles. They foraged from "first level" food sources such as wild game, fresh-caught fish from the sea or inland waterways, wild berries, nuts, and plant foods.

꙳

And out of the ground the LORD God made every tree grow that is pleasant to the sight and good for food.

—GENESIS 2:9

Be sure to include plenty of fruits and vegetables in your diet.

DAY 56

The biblical provision for food, as incorporated into the Maker's Diet, provides a great amount of vitamins, minerals, protein, healthy fats, and "phytochemicals" (the invaluable natural substances in plants that are neither vitamins nor minerals).

A wealth of nutrition awaits hurting bodies that are fed liberal doses of fruit, vegetables, herbs, lentils, and properly prepared whole grains (along with the meat, fish, and dairy products introduced later by the Creator).

꙳

And God said, "See, I have given you every herb that yields seed which is on the face of the earth, and every tree whose fruit yields seed; to you it shall be for food."

—GENESIS 1:29

Endurance activities (jogging, bicycling, swimming, or walking) combined with strength training are the best exercises for boosting long-term energy levels. Aim for forty-five to sixty minutes of exercise three to five times a week.

DAY 57

Members of my Jewish family have followed kosher dietary guidelines for generations—with a few exceptions. My grandmother always served her family kosher foods in the home but proudly declared, "The only place we eat *traife* (the Yiddish word for biblically unclean meats such as pork and shrimp) is at a Chinese restaurant." Grandma knew that pork and shrimp were biblically unclean foods, but she considered it acceptable to eat them as long as it was not in her home.

That logic did not change the potential ill effects of those meats, however. You will only receive the best God has for you if you obey His laws.

> *The pig has a split hoof, divided in two, but doesn't chew the cud and so is unclean....Make yourselves holy for I am holy.*
> —Leviticus 11:7, 44, The Message

Eat *fresh*, whole, unprocessed foods. Avoid empty-calorie, chemical-laden junk foods. They do nothing but satisfy a temporary craving. Real food satisfies your soul and truly nourishes your body.

DAY 58

When Dr. Weston A. Price analyzed the foods of isolated primitive peoples, he discovered that they provided at least four times the water-soluble vitamins, calcium, and other minerals and at least ten times the fat-soluble vitamins such as A, E, and D found in modern diets! The primitive diets derived these nutrients from animal foods such as butter, fatty fish, wild game, and organ meats.

For the word of the LORD is right, and all His work is done in truth.

—PSALM 33:4

Eat a light lunch. Loading up at lunch can leave you feeling tired, especially if you've eaten a carbohydrate-heavy meal of pasta, rice and beans, or bread. Eat a light or moderate lunch, and you'll have more energy in the afternoon.

DAY 59

Fully one-half of your nerve cells are located in the gut, so your capacity for feeling and for emotional expression depends primarily on the gut (and only to a lesser extent on your brain). By the time you add together the number of nerve cells in the esophagus, stomach, and small and large intestines, there are more nerve cells in the overall digestive system than there are in the peripheral nervous system.

For God is my record, how greatly I long after you in all the bowels of Jesus Christ.

—PHILIPPIANS 1:8, KJV

Eat five to ten servings per day of berries, fruits, vegetables, and melons; they are low in calories and high in energizing nutrients.

DAY 60

We tend to take our gut for granted, and it costs us dearly. We continually eat wrong foods that are rarely

digested properly. The by-products of incomplete digestion clog the gut with accumulated debris. This coating
becomes a perfect breeding ground for dangerous forms of
bacteria and other microorganisms.

But there is still good news! There are some very
positive things we can do to reverse any damage that has
already been done.

> *He who has health, has hope; and he who has*
> *hope, has everything.*
>
> —ARABIAN PROVERB

Drink ginger tea to combat energy drops, colds, flu, motion sickness, and gas pain.

DAY 61

We have come a long way in modern medicine. We now
know that the body's immune system is an autonomic
or "automatic" function. The body reacts automatically
when it senses an invasion by the disease-causing bacteria, fungi, viruses, and allergens that surround us in our
homes, job sites, or backyards. Thank God that He has
designed our bodies to fend off these enemies—sometimes
even before they attack!

> *For You formed my inward parts; You covered me*
> *in my mother's womb.*
>
> —PSALM 139:13

Learn to listen to the messages your body gives you.

DAY 62

We have just begun to harvest the vast resources of biological "bugs," and the search for new "super antibiotics" is growing more intense. Yet it seems the pool of known antibiotic formulas is growing less and less effective in the face of ever-mutating "super bugs" and infectious diseases.

The common approach to hygiene has classified all germs (microbes) as bad. Actually, the Creator designed our bodies to maximize use of naturally occurring substances in our environment—including microbes or "germs."

So you shall serve the LORD your God, and He will bless your bread and your water. And I will take sickness away from the midst of you.

—EXODUS 23:25

Avoid taking antibiotics if at all possible. Most minor medical problems can be alleviated by natural remedies.

DAY 63

Technology may be expanding exponentially, but nature is not. We are a part of God's natural creation, so most of us will benefit by returning the missing soil microorganisms to our bodies.

People should be made to understand that they must take charge of their own lives. Don't just take your body to the doctor as if he were a repair shop.

—QUENTIN REGESTEIN, SLEEP EXPERT
AND AUTHOR

High in natural sugar, ripe bananas are storehouses of quick, healthy energy. They are a good source of potassium, magnesium, fiber, and vitamins B and C. Consume a few of these energy-boosting fruits each week.

DAY 64

Chlorine continues to kill *all* bacteria—even the "good guys" inside our bodies. We're drinking an indiscriminate killer with the government's blessing. Populations in countries with low rates of asthma still drink water with billions of mycobacteria per liter. While I wouldn't advocate drinking impure water, I do recommend reconstituting the bacteria in your body in some other manner.

> *The Nation that destroys its soil and pollutes its water destroys itself.*
> —Franklin D. Roosevelt

Eating yogurt or cottage cheese is an excellent way to reconstitute the bacteria in your body's digestive system.

DAY 65

Contrary to the popular notion that "ignorance is bliss," where your health is concerned ignorance can be costly at best and deadly at worst. Digestive diseases and other conditions related to unhealthy intestinal flora imbalances have an enormous impact on our health and the nation's financial bottom line as well.

New technologies and new drugs have revolutionized the understanding and treatment of peptic ulcer disease and gastrointestinal esophageal reflux disease (GERD). Everyone hopes that *future* research will reduce the economic and health-care costs related to diagnosing and treating digestive diseases. But I believe we could benefit right now by tapping proven wisdom from the *past*.

> *Many people treat their bodies as if they were rented from Hertz—something they are using to get around in, but nothing they genuinely care about understanding.*
> —CHUNGLIANG AL HUANG, FITNESS EXPERT

Don't be ignorant about your body! Find a doctor who both appreciates and takes the time to answer your questions.

DAY 66

Even though they were virtually unknown just two hundred years ago, we now know that invisible organisms, both good and bad, play vital roles in our health—or our destruction. Bacteria can be either good or bad, and so the key is to maintain the correct balance between both in our bodies.

> *Health is not like the lottery. We are not just randomly stricken with disease. While some health outcomes are completely beyond our control, many diseases are affected by our decisions and behaviors.*
> —DAVID GIVEN, AUTHOR

Drink at least eight glasses of water each day to flush out your system and restore balance in the body.

DAY 67

Typically, human beings in virtually every culture engaged in the anaerobic type of functional exercise common to regular labor or work functions on the farm, at sea, or while hunting wild game. Long-distance walking or slower-paced labor functions may have been punctuated by intense but relatively brief bursts of physical labor or high-speed movement.

The sovereign invigorator of the body is exercise,
and of all the exercises, walking is the best.
—THOMAS JEFFERSON

Some aerobic exercise is acceptable, but your primary exercise activity should be anaerobic, not aerobic.

DAY 68

The simple reason the Maker's Diet can positively affect so many different health problems is that it improves the health of the entire body, especially the *digestive tract*, which affects virtually all other bodily systems. The healing of the digestive system in turn positively affects the immune system, endocrine system, heart, lungs, blood supply, brain, and total nervous system.

This proven health protocol involves a conscious return to the proteins, fats, carbohydrates, and additional micronutrients originally provided by our Creator for His highest creation, mankind.

Everything should be made as simple as possible,
but not simpler.
—ALBERT EINSTEIN

Eat two servings a day of foods like tomatoes; leafy green vegetables such as spinach and romaine lettuce; pinto, navy, or kidney beans; and grain products to decrease the levels of an amino acid that contributes to the process underlying heart disease and stroke.

DAY 69

Saturated fats are not the "dietary demons" behind modern diseases. The truth—according to the Bible, anthropological evidence from past civilizations, and recent scientific research—makes it clear that saturated fats play a crucial role in body chemistry.

The art of dining well is no slight art, the pleasure not a slight pleasure.
—MICHEL DE MONTAIGNE, FRENCH
RENAISSANCE THINKER

Eat foods that are high in saturated fats to help protect your liver from many toxins, including alcohol.

DAY 70

For thousands of years before the birth of America's corporate processed food giants, Americans ate foods barely one step from their natural state as the Creator intended. Vegetables were harvested from the garden just outside the back door and prepared for the table; fermented vegetables were enjoyed during the winter. Fruits were plucked from the family fruit trees and vines.

I no longer prepare food or drink with more than one ingredient.
—Cyra McFadden, American Journalist

Choose green, leafy lettuce, such as romaine lettuce, rather than iceberg lettuce, which has much less nutritional value.

DAY 71

Over 50 percent of the population takes vitamin or mineral supplements to improve energy and performance and to reduce the risk of deadly diseases such as cancer, heart disease, and diabetes.[23] However, despite widespread use of vitamin and mineral supplements since their introduction only fifty years ago, the incidence of major diseases has skyrocketed! Even more surprising is the lack of scientific research showing the efficacy of multivitamin/mineral supplements.

The preservation of health is a duty.
—Herbert Spencer, Victorian English
Philosopher

Choose *homeostatic nutrients,* which, unlike most nutritional supplements on the market, provide vitamins and minerals in the natural form our Creator intended—as living food.

DAY 72

Figs are mentioned more than fifty times in the Bible and are the first fruit specifically named in Scripture (Gen. 3:7). Whether fresh or dried, figs have been prized since ancient times for their sweetness and nutritional value.

Grapes were the first crop Noah planted after the Flood. They were made into wine and vinegar or eaten fresh or dried.

❧

And Noah began to be a farmer, and he planted a vineyard.

—GENESIS 9:20

Grapes fight tooth decay, stop viruses in their tracks, and are rich in other ingredients that many researchers believe may lower risk of cancer.

DAY 73

Seeds, already rich sources of nutrients, become real nutritional powerhouses when they are soaked and sprouted. The germination process (sprouting) produces vitamin C and increases carotenoids and vitamin B content, especially B_2, B_5, and B_6. Even more importantly, sprouting neutralizes phytic acid, a substance present in the bran of all seeds that inhibits the absorption of calcium, magnesium, iron, and zinc.

❧

Life is not merely being alive, but being well.
—MARTIAL, ROMAN PHILOSOPHER

Opt for bean sprouts on sandwiches or in salads as frequently as possible.

DAY 74

Stress comes at you from at least four sources:

1. Outward circumstances over which you have *no* control

2.   Circumstances or influences over which you *do* have control

3.   *Inward* attitudes, beliefs, and thought patterns

4.   Internal *physical* conditions

For maximum health, it is important to become skilled in handling stress according to the Creator's principles.

A man becomes what he thinks about all day long.

—Ralph Waldo Emerson

To help reduce stress, determine the factors over which you *do* have control, and begin to manage those areas.

DAY 75

Cortisol is a steroid hormone that affects your body in ways very similar to prednisone—it blocks inflammation and suppresses the immune system. DHEA is the balancing hormone that reverses the effects of cortisol. (DHEA has antiaging effects, boosts the immune system, and exerts key influence on sex hormones—thus, fertility.)[24] One of the important keys to achieve a healthy life is to eat a diet and live a lifestyle that promote a healthy balance of DHEA and cortisol. When these two hormones are in balance, we experience excellent health physically, mentally, and emotionally.

Remember the Sabbath day, to keep it holy. Six days you shall labor and do all your work, but

the seventh day is the Sabbath of the LORD your God.

—EXODUS 20:8–10

The Sabbath is important, not only as a day of rest, but as a day of freedom from stress.

DAY 76

Dr. Michael Miller from the University of Maryland told attendees at an American Heart Association Conference, "We don't know why laughter protects the heart.... We know that exercising, not smoking and eating foods low in saturated fat will reduce the risk of heart disease. Perhaps regular hearty laughter should be added to the list."[25]

The [doctor's] recommendations for a healthy heart may one day be exercise, eat right and laugh a few times a day!
—DR. MICHAEL MILLER, MEDICAL CONSULTANT

My own professional opinion? "You gotta laugh a little!"

DAY 77

When I started to *believe* I was well and to give thanks to God for the *moments* of well-being I experienced, I began to get well. The memorable moment when I asked my mother to take my picture at 111 pounds, when I was barely able to stand, demonstrated the seed of faith that sparked my healing. It was that mustard seed of faith that eventually moved the mountain of illness in my life.

Collaborate with nature. Value beauty. Create an environment that entices good fortune.
—VICTORIA MORAN, AUTHOR, SPEAKER, HUMORIST

Keep a daily log of your improvement: your dietary changes, as well as any positive signs of wellness that are occurring in your body. When you need encouragement, glance back at how far you've come.

DAY 78

The longest-lived peoples in human history usually walked everywhere they went, trailed their animals and herds, hunted wild game on foot, built rugged shelters, or cultivated fields at an active pace each day with intermittent periods of rest. They knew *nothing* about aerobic exercise, treadmills, or running tracks, but they were masters at *anaerobic exercise*—activities that incur an "oxygen debt" through temporary or briefly sustained exertion.

God will bring the vision He has given you to reality in your life if you will wait on His timing.
—OSWALD CHAMBERS, CHRISTIAN AUTHOR

Anyone can certainly be a lot healthier with a nutritious diet and moderate exercise.

DAY 79

One way to get the exercise you need is rebounding, in which you use a portable mini-trampoline to jog, jump, hop, twist, or step walk in place.

According to James White, PhD, director of research

and rehabilitation in the physical education department of the University of California at San Diego (UCSD), "When you jump, jog and twist on this [rebounder] device, you can exercise for hours without getting tired. It's great practice for skiing, it improves your tennis stroke, and it's a good way to burn off calories and lose weight."[26] Dr. White believes it is more effective for fitness and weight loss than cycling, running, or jogging—while producing fewer injuries.

> *One of the basic causes of illness is unhappiness,*
> *and one of the greatest healers is joy.*
> —STEPHANIE TOURLES, SELF-HELP AUTHOR

If you are stuck indoors, try some "rebounding" exercise in which you jump on a mini-trampoline.

DAY 80

Natural herbs still offer us medicines for inducing healing, preserving health, and improving our quality of life. Many of these herbs are used as seasonings; some are edible in salads or soups; and some can be used to make teas. It is very beneficial to incorporate these wonderful substances into your everyday diet.

> *Ignoring your daily health habits does not make*
> *any sense and will not help you today, tomorrow,*
> *or down the road. When you are hungry you eat,*
> *but before you are hungry you plan how to get*
> *food. It should be the same way with your health.*
> *When you are sick you see a doctor, but before*
> *you are sick you should plan on how to be well.*
> —DR. JENNIFER PETERSON, AUTHOR

Begin gradually adding herbs to your diet, especially the top twenty-one listed later in this book, and see how they can begin to improve your life.

DAY 81

In the Middle Ages, Jewish spice merchants' hands were dyed yellow from saffron, so they were often called "saffron merchants." Saffron yellow was used to mock Jews for centuries, but never so cruelly as by Nazi Germany's requirement that all Jews wear armbands bearing a yellow Star of David.

Saffron was used medically in tinctures for treating gastric and intestinal problems and is considered an antispasmodic, an expectorant, a sedative, and a stimulant in small doses.[27]

Go confidently in the direction of your dreams. Live the life you've imagined.
—HENRY DAVID THOREAU

Take saffron as a preventative measure against bladder, kidney, and liver ailments.

DAY 82

We would think it foolish for someone to squander a free membership to an exclusive health spa or exclusive golf country club. Yet how often do we take the time to partake of God's bounty of healing herbs, essential oils, the relaxation of a soothing hot bath, and soothing and inspirational music?

The worth of every conviction consists precisely in the steadfastness in which it is held.

—JANE ADDAMS, FOUNDER OF THE
WORLD-FAMOUS SOCIAL SETTLEMENT
HULL HOUSE IN CHICAGO IN 1889

If you sense it is time for a significant change in your life, it is most likely to happen with a clear-cut decision and a period of commitment.

DAY 83

Under primitive conditions, food is vital for survival; primitive people "ate to live." In our era, we have allowed food to become our idol. Too many people admittedly "live to eat."

Most modern men and women have strayed far from the Creator's foods, the same foods that traditionally nourished the world's healthiest people. In our promiscuous society, we say *yes* to virtually every whim and desire of our palate, resulting in a national dilemma of becoming an overweight, sedentary, and increasingly sick population.

The good news is that it is not too late to change. And while you may not be able to change America's eating habits, you can certainly change your own!

But the fruit of the Spirit is . . . self-control.
—GALATIANS 5:22–23

Ask for God's help to learn to control your eating habits.

DAY 84

In an odd twist of logic, many religious Americans dismiss the Jewish dietary laws as outdated legalism, invalid for the modern era. Yet they embrace the fundamental truths of the Ten Commandments as universal and timeless. Shouldn't we at least consider the Creator's dietary guidelines in the same way?

> *Only be strong and very courageous, that you may observe to do according to all the law which Moses My servant commanded you; do not turn from it to the right hand or to the left, that you may prosper wherever you go.*
>
> —JOSHUA 1:7

Lifting weights enhances your metabolism. Try to fit in a weight workout two or three times a week.

DAY 85

Some of us diligently verify the claims on prepackaged food reassuring us they are "enriched with 12 vitamins" or that they are "100 percent natural."

The unfortunate truth is that most prepackaged and fast-food products overload our bodies with adulterated fats and refined sugars such as those found in candy, baked goods, and refined grains. That includes the innocuous hamburger buns and "wholesome bread" wrapped around our "low-fat" grilled chicken breasts.

Should we give up and just eat twigs, leaves, and berries the rest of our lives? No, we don't have to be that extreme. There is a better way! The Maker's Diet.

*He will teach us His ways, and we shall walk in
His paths.*

—ISAIAH 2:3

To boost your brainpower, eat high-protein snacks, such as peanut butter, sesame butter, or cottage cheese.

DAY 86

For many years health practitioners (and most people with a dose of common sense) have understood the importance of good nutrition for mothers during pregnancy. Dr. Weston A. Price's research revealed that members of primitive cultures have long understood and practiced "preconception nutritional programs" for both prospective parents—mothers and fathers. The Maker's Diet is beneficial for both men and women—and their future children.

*Marvelous are Your works, and that my soul
knows very well. My frame was not hidden from
You, when I was made in secret, and skillfully
wrought in the lowest parts of the earth.*

—PSALM 139:14–15

Young men and women who are planning to have children should begin the Maker's Diet to help ensure a healthy baby—as well as healthy parents!

DAY 87

People are taught from childhood to believe that the brain is essentially the "boss" of the body. While it is true that the brain is the centerpiece of our mental capacity and nervous system, it is also a fact that there are nearly one hundred million nerve cells in the gut alone—about the same number found in the spinal cord!

Most people would say the brain determines whether you are happy or sad, but they have their facts skewed. It seems the gut is more responsible than we ever imagined for mental well-being and how we *feel*.

Put on therefore, as the elect of God, holy and beloved, bowels of mercies, kindness, humbleness of mind, meekness, longsuffering.
—COLOSSIANS 3:12, KJV

The next time you have a "gut feeling" about something, you might think about following it—more often than not, it is probably right!

DAY 88

The "gut" is fully self-contained and yet intricately dependent and interlinked with every other major system of your body. It is becoming clearer that anything that exerts an influence on the body—i.e., swimming and showering in chlorinated water, using fluoride toothpaste, wearing synthetic clothing, or even cleaning house with powerful chemicals—may indirectly or directly affect your gut and therefore your health. On the other hand, avoiding these things will also affect your health—but in a positive way!

The greatest wealth is health.
—VIRGIL, ROMAN EPIC POET

If you must brush your teeth with fluoride toothpaste, avoid swallowing any of it.

DAY 89

We also now understand that germs don't fly—they hitchhike. Germs generally travel via hand-to-hand contact or hand-to-surface-to-hand transfer. Your hands come into contact with the chief agents of infection on hundreds of surfaces daily, including other hands (and whatever they have touched).

More than 90 percent of the germs on your hands reside under your fingernails. The same is true for allergens and environmental contaminants.

The human body has been designed to resist an infinite number of changes and attacks brought about by its environment. The secret of good health lies in successful adjustment to changing stresses on the body.

—Harry J. Johnson, American Doctor

To reduce allergens in your bedroom, launder your bedsheets in hot water twice a week.

DAY 90

Every day scientists fan out around the globe with spoons and sandwich bags in hand looking for new sources of soil microorganisms in bat caves, jungle clearings, peat bogs, hot springs, undersea volcanoes, and even from mummies. Each exotic locale may yield a completely new discovery of germs—a gold mine of potential pharmaceutical profits.

Some leading government officials and scientists in the United States suspect that organisms in our soil may yield powerful new treatments for AIDS, cancer, and other deadly diseases.

Honour a physician with the honour due unto him...for the Lord hath created him.

—ECCLESIASTICUS 38:1, THE APOCRYPHA

Schedule a yearly physical with your family doctor to maintain good health throughout your lifetime.

DAY 91

So-called enlightened parents do everything they can today to keep Junior from getting "dirty." The sad truth is that our environment is too clean! Immune cells that do not have adequate exposure to soil microbes tend to over-react when they do come into contact with them. Too many adults and children have been denied this much-needed exposure to soil microorganisms. The immune systems of children and even adults are overreactive because they are no longer being properly "educated" in the biological playground of life.

Forget not that the earth delights to feel your bare feet upon it.

—KAHLIL GIBRAN, AUTHOR

Allow your children to play outside as much as they can.

DAY 92

Antibiotics kill both good and bad bacteria. Even if you don't take antibiotics, you almost certainly consume them in animal products. United States pharmaceutical firms produce more than 35 million pounds of antibiotics each year, and animals receive the vast bulk of them.

Growers routinely give big helpings of antibiotics to cattle, pigs, and poultry to prevent infections from spreading in their stressful, crowded quarters. It is so bad that the European Common Market refuses to import livestock from American farms.

> *The whole of nature, as has been said, is a conjugation of the verb "to eat," in the active and the passive.*
> —ROBERT G. INGERSOLL, AMERICAN ORATOR

In your local health food grocery store ask for meat that has not been tainted by antibiotics.

DAY 93

Your body desperately requires healthy intestinal flora because your health depends on it. A healthy gastrointestinal system has a balance of approximately 85 percent "good" bacteria to 15 percent "bad" microorganisms. Unfortunately, most of us show the reverse ratio. If our ignorance about hygiene contributes to the problem, then we should determine to educate ourselves. The benefits we reap will be immense.

> *Few seem conscious that there is such a thing as physical mortality, and fewer still take steps to avoid it.*
> —HERBERT SPENCER, VICTORIAN ENGLISH
> PHILOSOPHER

Commit to hygienic practices in the kitchen—not letting food sit out, wiping down countertops with a cleanser, and not cross-contaminating food such as raw chicken with vegetables.

DAY 94

There are three simple steps to guard our health from the bad guy bacteria and strengthen it with the good guy bacteria:

1. First, we balance the double-edged sword of hygiene by cleansing rather than sterilizing our bodies (particularly under the fingernails and around the eyes and nasal passages), using advanced hygiene. This permits exposure to the environment without overload.

2. Second, we feed our bodies healthy living foods from the Maker's Diet.

3. Third, we repopulate and strengthen the living environment in the gut with soil-based organisms (SBOs).

The human body is not a thing or a substance given, but a continuous creation. It is an energy system which is never a complete structure; it is in perpetual inner self-destruction and self-construction.
—NORMAN O. BROWN, PHILOSOPHER AND CRITIC

Begin to put these three steps into practice in your life, and watch your health dramatically improve.

DAY 95

Conventional medicine sends its troops into battle against disease armed solely with surgery, pharmaceuticals, and invasive therapies like chemotherapy and radiation. Anything outside the ironclad realm of a knife, a pill, or an

X-ray machine is considered voodoo or worse. The genuine "maintenance" of health is simply beyond the scope of this "take-two-tablets-and-call-me-in-the-morning" philosophy.

🐟

God heals, and the doctor takes the fee.
—BENJAMIN FRANKLIN

Whether choosing an over-the-counter medicine or receiving a prescription from your doctor, ask whether the medicine is meant for someone in your precise medical situation.

DAY 96

Just one hundred years ago or less, the diet of the average American was dramatically different from our standard American table fare today. Widespread corporate "mono-agriculture" with concentration on single-crop specialties and chemical fertilizers and pesticides was unheard of then, so the typical diet consisted mostly of fruit; vegetables; wild grain and seeds; fish; raw, unpasteurized dairy products; and meat from wild animals.

🐟

We are indeed much more than what we eat, but what we eat can nevertheless help us to be much more than what we are.
—ADELLE DAVIS, NUTRITIONIST

Eating fish three to four times each week will provide your body with its needed omega-3 oils to help prevent disease.

DAY 97

The Maker's Diet focuses on the balanced intake of *natural* fats occurring in ocean-caught fish; cod liver oil; omega-3 eggs; and grass-fed, organic, and free-range meats. It also includes animal products such as butter, cheeses, and full-fat lacto-fermented dairy products like yogurt and kefir, as well as raw milk and cream from goats, sheep, cows, and other biblically "clean" mammals.

Food is our common ground, a universal experience.

—JAMES BEARD, AMERICAN CHEF
AND FOOD WRITER

Eat 4 ounces of fish (think one small can of tuna) two to four times a week to cut your risk of stroke.

DAY 98

The Maker's recommended fiber sources, the kind of fiber that promotes colon health, are found in *low-carbohydrate,* high-fiber foods. These foods include broccoli, cauliflower, celery, and lettuce, as well as soaked or sprouted seeds, nuts, grains, and legumes. Besides providing the right kind of fiber, these foods are rich in vitamins, minerals, and antioxidants.

Go, eat your bread with joy, and drink your wine with a merry heart.

—ECCLESIASTES 9:7

Berries and other small fruit, along with fruit and vegetables with edible skins, are good sources of low-carbohydrate fiber.

DAY 99

More and more, history and science are confirming that the Creator's provisions for mankind's need for food are still the best choices for ensuring health and quality of life today.

There are seven "macrominerals" (calcium, chloride, magnesium, phosphorus, potassium, sodium, and sulfur) and at least thirty trace minerals that are essential to life. If present in only minute amounts, these minerals prevent certain diseases and promote proper body function.

May your soil be blessed with peace, where life in all its forms will comfort you.

—ANONYMOUS

Be sure to eat nutrient-rich foods, beverages, broths, and living multivitamins with homeostatic nutrients.

DAY 100

While not mentioned explicitly in the Bible, *berries* are super foods containing some of the highest levels of antioxidants known to man. Blueberries contain antioxidant compounds that show promise in reversing some of the effects of aging, especially the loss of cognitive function.

Make the most of yourself, for that is all there is of you.

—ANONYMOUS

Blueberries, strawberries, blackberries, and raspberries make a great, healthy addition to any diet.

DAY 101

High omega-3 eggs are nature's nearly perfect food. Eggs contain *all known nutrients except for vitamin C!* They are good sources of fat-soluble vitamins A and D as well as certain carotenoids that guard against free-radical damage to the body. They also contain lutein, which has been shown to prevent age-related macular degeneration.

> *Moving toward a simple life is not about deprivation or denying ourselves the things we want. It's about getting rid of the things that no longer contribute to the fullness of our lives. It's about creating balance between our inner and outer lives.*
> —DAVID GIVEN, AUTHOR

When possible, buy eggs directly from farms where the chickens are allowed to roam free and eat their natural diet, or purchase eggs marked DHA or high omega-3 eggs (they contain a healthy balance of omega-3 to omega-6).

DAY 102

Anger, resentment, unforgiveness, and a desire for revenge all trigger the classic "alarm triad" response to stress, which involves adrenal gland hypertrophy (swelling), thymus and lymph gland atrophy (shrinkage), indicating the suppression of the immune system, and gastric inflammation.

> *Peter came to Him [Jesus] and said, "Lord, how often shall my brother sin against me, and I forgive him? Up to seven times?" Jesus said to him, "I do not say to you, up to seven times, but up to seventy times seven."*
> —MATTHEW 18:21–22

Practice forgiveness as a way of life, not just a one-time event.

DAY 103

These age-old "life-shorteners" were well documented in Scripture long before scientists and researchers set out to quantify the effects of negative emotions on our bodies. At last we are beginning to catch up to the Creator's wisdom.

Is it really worth the dangerous cost to hold on to anger or unforgiveness? Are you really willing to destroy yourself in a quest for revenge?

Forgive, and you will be forgiven.

—LUKE 6:37

For your own sake and the sake of your health, let go of any grudges you may be holding.

DAY 104

A seemingly far-fetched, ridiculous-sounding, positive thought, word, or action that you can choose to express in your moment of desperation can act as a seed of faith that will spark the healing process for you.

Faith is the substance of things hoped for, the evidence of things not seen.

—HEBREWS 11:1

As you meditate on God's Word and pray, daring to quote His promises for your healing, your faith will grow, and you will receive your miracle.

DAY 105

Elementary schoolchildren hear it over and over again: "If your clothing catches fire, just *stop, drop, and roll!*" This fire safety formula has some genuine application to the problem of physical, mental, and spiritual burnout as well.

When it comes to your health, if you sense the heat of life on your backside and smell the smoke of imminent burnout billowing around you, just stop, drop, and roll—more literally, *rest*, *fast*, and *exercise*.

> *I pray for good fortune in everything you do, and for your good health—that your everyday affairs prosper, as well as your soul!*
> —3 John 2, The Message

Getting the proper amount of sleep, fasting from certain foods, and exercising regularly will greatly improve your health.

DAY 106

My description of the oldest physical activity of the human race can be expressed in one word: *walking*. Even before Eve, Adam was assigned the task to care for God's garden—a job that could not be done without *walking*. Subsequent development of our species demanded even more walking.

> *In the long run, men hit only what they aim at.*
> —Henry David Thoreau

A brisk two-mile walk (with long strides and vigorous arm movement) every day increases enzyme and metabolic activity and may increase calorie burning for up to twelve hours afterward![28]

DAY 107

We are much less active than we used to be, but even a little exercise goes a long way. Researchers have proven that the greatest benefit of beginning an exercise program occurred between the most unfit volunteers and those who were just slightly more fit.[29]

Regardless of where you land on the exercise scale, this should make you feel better. Even if you don't exercise at all, you can begin to improve your health immediately by starting to exercise now.

❧

Those who think they have not time for bodily exercise will sooner or later have to find time for illness.

—EDWARD STANLEY, NINETEENTH-CENTURY AUTHOR

Simply starting an exercise program and finding out what works for you can improve your health almost immediately.

DAY 108

Aloe vera purges the stomach and lower intestines when taken internally (exercise caution here), and it aids the healing of open sores. It has anesthetic and antibacterial properties and literally increases blood or lymph flow in small vessels where it is applied topically. Use it for teenage acne, too.

❧

Self-esteem is about trusting your ability to make appropriate choices and cope effectively with adversity.

—NATHANIAL BRANDEN, PSYCHOLOGIST

Try heating an actual aloe vera leaf and applying it directly to abscesses, bruises, skin inflammations, gumboils, or even sprains.

DAY 109

Black cumin oil contains *nigellone*, which protects guinea pigs from histamine-induced bronchial spasms (perhaps explaining its use to relieve the symptoms of asthma, bronchitis, and coughs). The presence of the antitumor sterol, beta sitosterol, lends some credence to its use in folklore to treat abscesses and tumors of the abdomen, eyes, and liver.[30]

The nearer the bone, the sweeter the meat.
—ENGLISH PROVERB

For healthy digestive function, occasionally use black cumin oil when cooking.

DAY 110

The spikenard's rhizome, or large root, contains jatamansi, a compound used to treat epilepsy. Infusions are used to treat epilepsy, hysteria, heart palpitations, and chorea. Spikenard oil may help treat auricular flutter, and it acts to depress the central nervous system and relax skeletal and soft tissue muscles.[31]

As we begin to pry ourselves loose from our old self-concepts, we find that our new, emerging self may enjoy all sorts of adventures.
—JULIA CAMERON, AUTHOR

Spikenard oil may be used to treat irregular heartbeats.

DAY 111

I encourage you to tap into the power of the Maker's music and allow it to drain away stress, build up your soul, and enhance your health. It is a divine tool from the loving hand of God to make everyday life a little healthier.

Music is well said to be the speech of angels.
—THOMAS CARLYLE, BRITISH HISTORIAN

The right music at the right time can calm you, excite you, awaken you, or put you to sleep.

DAY 112

The top ten leading causes of hospitalizations and insurance claims in the United States in 1990 included obesity, diabetes, hemorrhoids (or varicose veins), heart attacks, diverticulosis and diverticulitis, cancer, peptic ulcer, hiatal hernia, appendicitis, and gallstones.[32]

These represent diseases of lifestyle, revealing the hazardous effects of civilization, which are expanding as modernization spreads to more of the world's nations and cultures. However, these diseases are still uncommon among primitive people groups today, and history indicates they were virtually unknown among the oldest primitive civilizations.

It is hope that maintains most of mankind.
—SOPHOCLES

Be aware of your family's history of or propensity toward certain diseases so that you can purposely avoid increasing your risk of developing them yourself.

DAY 113

God's moral guidelines preserved spiritual purity, social order, family stability, and community prosperity. While the moral guidelines preserved the culture of Israel, the dietary guidelines preserved their physical health. God's dietary guidelines are not some narrow-minded religious exercise meant to set apart certain people from their neighbors. They were given by a loving God to save His people from physical devastation long before scientific principles of hygiene, viral transmission, bacterial infection, or molecular cell physiology were understood!

You are a holy people to the Lord your God, and the Lord has chosen you to be a people for Himself, a special treasure above all the peoples who are on the face of the earth.

—Deuteronomy 14:2

Peanut butter is a great high-energy, on-the-go snack.

DAY 114

The Maker's Diet is a comprehensive lifestyle plan that will help you choose a better way. The simple biblical principles I have incorporated into this plan can spare you the misery of debilitating modern diseases and health crises such as arthritis, cancer, obesity, diabetes, heart attack, and stroke—or help you recover from them.

He causes the grass to grow for the cattle, and vegetation for the service of man, that he may bring forth food from the earth.

—Psalm 104:14

Spice up your life with naturally fermented relishes and condiments instead of sugary sauce substitutes.

DAY 115

Dr. Weston A. Price learned that many primitive tribes required a period of premarital nutrition for youth who were planning to wed. Special foods were often given to maturing boys and girls in preparation for future parenthood, as well as to pregnant and lactating women. Dr. Price found these foods to be very rich in fat-soluble vitamins A and D—nutrients found only in animal fats.

> *The secret things belong to the LORD our God, but those things which are revealed belong to us and to our children forever, that we may do all the words of this law.*
> —DEUTERONOMY 29:29

Feed your children healthy foods from the Maker's Diet instead of the junk food that most of America's youth consume.

DAY 116

Do you remember the gut sensation of what we call "butterflies in your stomach"? Has anyone ever advised you to "follow your gut instinct"? We regularly hear people say their stomach indigestion caused nightmares, and patients often tell their doctors that the antidepressants they take for mood swings also lessened their gastrointestinal symptoms.

The "second brain" in your gut can *act independently* from the first brain in your body. It learns from experiences, remembers past actions and events, and produces an entire range of "gut feelings" that can influence your actions.

Negative emotions drain your enthusiasm and zest for life, but a positive attitude is refreshing and contagious.

—Anonymous

Surround yourself with people who are happy and have a strong sense of purpose.

DAY 117

Virtually every state of health is affected by the GI (gastrointestinal) tract. Even if you break a bone or undergo a surgical procedure, the time required to heal is directly affected by how well your gut is able to process nutrients and detoxify toxins!

And even if you are the most intelligent person in the world, if you fail to fuel your body properly, your brilliant intellect may be dimmed or extinguished through poor nutrition and poor lifestyle decisions. On the other hand, if your body is in shape, your potential in every other area of life will soar.

Health is a state of complete physical, mental, and social well-being, and not merely the absence of disease or infirmity.

—World Health Organization

Be sure to eat a well-balanced breakfast, especially on days you know will be mentally or emotionally taxing.

DAY 118

Unfortunately, it is difficult to reach germs under the fingernails with normal hand-washing techniques. And these germs easily enter the body through the nasal passageways or the tear ducts of the eyes when we touch them—which occurs at least twenty times a day. Typically, your fingertips come in contact with your eyes and nose more than 12,500 times each year. Each time there is the potential of autoinoculating yourself with germs, allergens, environmental toxins, and viruses.

❧

Cleanliness is next to godliness.

—ANONYMOUS

Purchase a small nail brush. Use it to scrub under your fingernails with soap and hot water several times each week.

DAY 119

Why all the scientific excitement about dirt? Nothing fuels a worldwide hunt like the potential of finding treasure. In this case, the treasure is newly discovered microbes, different from any that have been used to date to create antibiotics. Many current antibiotics *come from microbes in the soil*, including streptomycin, the first treatment for tuberculosis, and vancomycin, currently the drug of last resort for the toughest infections.[33]

❧

If by gaining knowledge we destroy our health, we labour for a thing that will be useless in our hands.

—JOHN LOCKE, SEVENTEENTH-CENTURY
ENGLISH PHILOSOPHER

Pray that God gives the knowledge necessary to researchers to discover the cures for diseases. His will is that we are well!

DAY 120

We tend to oversterilize everything—with disinfectant dishwashing, hand soaps, and shower gels; disinfectant body lotions and skin bars; and "deodorant soaps" loaded with antibiotic disinfectants such as triclosan. And we sterilize our soil using pesticides and herbicides that destroy beneficial and harmful microbes alike. These agents harm even the natural immune systems of the very plants we try to "help" with our technological advances.

Better to hunt through fields outdoors for health than charge the doctor for useless medicine.
—JOHN DRYDEN, ENGLISH POET

Cleansing—our bodies, clothes, dishes, etc.—is important. Sterilization is not.

DAY 121

The intestine of a healthy child or adult normally contains billions of bacteria and other microorganisms from up to 10,000 different species. Ideally, the beneficial or benign *bacteria* in your body should outnumber the *cells* of your body by approximately one hundred to one. One side benefit of these friendly bacteria is that they also increase the body's levels of interferon, a powerful immunity-boosting chemical. These beneficial bacteria are your best friends!

Health is something we do for ourselves, not something that is done to us; a journey rather

than a destination; a dynamic, holistic, and
purposeful way of living.
—Dr. Elliott Dacher, Physician and Author

Listen to your body. If you eat when you're hungry and stop when you're satisfied, you'll naturally have plenty of energy. But if you eat until you're stuffed and don't listen to your body's signals of fullness, your energy will wane.

DAY 122

Steps to a healthy gut #1: Restore your connection to the soil. You may not be comfortable making mud pies with your children, so I recommend that you do a little gardening, hike in the mountains, or supplement your diet with homeostatic soil organisms. A growing number of scientists, nutritionists, and medical doctors are convinced that this is the most effective way to enhance the healing response of the body.

✽

Nature tops the list of potent tranquilizers and
stress reducers. The mere sound of moving water
has been shown to lower blood pressure.
—Patch Adams, Physician

Getting outdoors—back to Mother Nature—can be fun and relaxing as well as good for you!

DAY 123

Steps to a healthy gut #2: Reap the benefits of soil-based organism supplementation. Most people who begin SBO supplementation in concert with healthy dietary choices see a rapid and overall improvement in bodily functions and natural immunity to disease and infection.

The best six doctors anywhere
And no one can deny it
Are sunshine, water, rest, and air
Exercise and diet.
These six will gladly you attend
If only you are willing.
Your mind they'll ease
Your will they'll mend
And charge you not a shilling.
—Nursery Rhyme Quoted by Wayne Fields,
American Essayist

Consuming soil-based organisms in the form of a supplement is frequently more effective than trying to glean it from the environment.

DAY 124

Vitamins and minerals that have not been incorporated into an organic matrix—a natural food form containing all necessary cofactors—may actually be very harmful to the body. It is better to supplement healthy food and beverage choices with living food supplements known as homeostatic nutrients rich in vitamins and minerals. This is a balanced form the body can absorb and utilize.

Health is a large word. It embraces not the body only, but the mind and spirit as well...and not today's pain or pleasure alone, but the whole being and outlook of a man.
—James H. West, Author

Visit the Maker's Diet Web site (www.TMDiet.com) for information on specific brands of living food supplements.

DAY 125

Though "maintenance" of health is mentioned often in the world of allopathic or nonconventional medicine, the practical function of defining and preserving genuine good health is beyond the reach of most conventional medical doctors because of their consuming focus on the "cut, poison, and burn" approach to treating disease. Most medical doctors totally exclude basic nutrition from their treatment plans. Indeed, they have little educational background to do otherwise.

✣

> *To set a man's will against his sickness is the supreme art of medicine.*
> —HENRY WARD BEECHER, PROTESTANT CLERGYMAN AND REFORMER

The prevention of disease and the maintenance of health do not begin in the emergency room or the doctor's office; they begin with the lifestyle choices you make every day.

DAY 126

Since the Creator made us with a perpetual pattern in mind, it should not surprise us to discover that we crave the foods, in their natural state, that our ancestors consumed. Our physical bodies were engineered as marvelous, highly tuned machines, genetically set for nutritional requirements established from the beginning of time.

And the LORD God commanded the man, saying,
"Of every tree of the garden you may freely eat;
but of the tree of the knowledge of good and evil
you shall not eat."

—GENESIS 2:16–17

Chew slowly! Be conscious of each portion of food you put in your mouth, and put your fork down between bites.

DAY 127

Carbohydrates are the *starches* and *sugars* produced by all plants, synthesized by the body from proteins and fats, and "refined" by humans until they become "negative" calories that leach nutrients from the body rather than replace them.

Eat breakfast like a king, lunch like a prince, and
dinner like a pauper.

—ADELLE DAVIS, NUTRITIONIST

When cutting calories from your diet, do so in small increments: 50 here, 100 there, rather than one big lump.

DAY 128

One form of helpful fiber, called *mucilaginous* fiber, also helps relieve constipation and soothes inflamed tissue in the lining of the gut. In addition, toxins are more quickly flushed out of the body before they putrefy in the intestines.

Public and private food in America has become

eatable, here and there extremely good. Only the fried potatoes go unchanged, as deadly as before.

—LUIGI BARZINI, ITALIAN ESSAYIST

Get your mucilaginous fiber in chia and flaxseeds.

DAY 129

If you follow the precise biblical recommendations for the Creator's seafood, you can ensure health and avoid disease. Fish is a wonderfully rich source of protein, potassium, vitamins, and minerals. Today we understand scientifically that fish and cod liver oil thin the blood, protect the arteries from damage, and lower blood pressure.

🐟

Learn to love your body in all its strengths and weaknesses.

—STEPHANIE TOURLES, SELF-HELP AUTHOR

For those who simply don't get enough cold-water fish, it is imperative that you take a form of high-quality cod liver oil every day.

DAY 130

Stocks and soups appear in biblical diets, and meat and fish stocks are virtually universal fixtures in traditional cuisine in France, Italy, China, Japan, Africa, South America, Russia, and the Middle East. Chicken soup is popular in Western cultures, while fish soup enjoys the same reputation in the Orient and South America.

The winds of grace are blowing all the time, and
it's up to us to raise our sails.
—FATHER THOMAS KEATING, AUTHOR

Chicken soup, widely considered a "cure-all," is sometimes called *Jewish penicillin* because it is effective against many minor illnesses we all face from time to time.

DAY 131

Fermented vegetables such as sauerkraut, pickled carrots, beets, or cucumbers are some of the most health-giving foods on the planet. Raw cultured or fermented vegetables provide the body with beneficial microorganisms known as probiotics and an abundance of enzymes. They are also a rich source of many vitamins, including vitamin C, and are very easy to digest. Sauerkraut (fermented cabbage) contains nearly four times the cancer-fighting nutrients as unfermented cabbage and is the primary source of vegetable nutrition in many countries where the winters are cold.

Ill health, of body or of mind, is defeat. Health
alone is victory. Let all men, if they can manage
it, contrive to be healthy!
—THOMAS CARLYLE, BRITISH HISTORIAN

Cultured/fermented vegetables are very easy to make and are readily available at health food stores everywhere. Try some!

DAY 132

When it comes to stress, it seems that the body can handle the day-to-day emergencies and surprises without any problem—but when stress hangs on, it drains the adrenal system, making a "crash" inevitable.

In contrast, studies have shown that people "who experienced an episode of deep appreciation or love for five minutes saw their IgA levels (an antibody secreted in saliva and other body fluids as a first line of defense against infection) rise to 40 percent above normal and stay elevated for six hours."[34]

Beloved, let us love one another, for love is of God; and everyone who loves is born of God and knows God.

—1 JOHN 4:7

Hug someone today—it's good for you!

DAY 133

Even simple lifestyle adjustments can make a significant difference in your stress levels. A ringing phone causes stress in many people—some more than others. The constant demands of the workplace can be carried into the home environment if they are not purposefully left at the door.

True life is lived when tiny changes occur.
—LEO TOLSTOY, AUTHOR

If you frequently feel too busy to get away from the telephone or cell phone, then your stress-buster may be an answering service or simply the "off" switch on your phone.

DAY 134

Just as the original manufacturer of an automobile provides detailed information and maintenance schedules for maintaining maximum performance and utility of that car, so your Creator has provided detailed instructions and maintenance schedules for preserving peak performance for you.

And He [God] said, "My Presence will go with you, and I will give you rest."

—EXODUS 33:14

Even if you're so active that your friends confuse you with the Energizer bunny, you still need regular periods of rest.

DAY 135

Every working creature needs a Sabbath rest—that goes for people, animals, and even the soil! People and animals need a break every seven days, and even the soil prospers with a break at least every seven years. Every wise farmer understands the need to put fields and crops in rotation so the soil can replenish at least one growing season every seven years.

Work shall be done for six days, but the seventh day shall be a holy day for you, a Sabbath of rest to the LORD.

—EXODUS 35:2

Reserve Sunday for God and yourself. Worship Him at church, but rest for the remainder of the day.

DAY 136

Don't waste time looking for choice parking spots close to your destination—choose a spot far away and walk there. This takes care of two important priorities at once—you get what you came for, and you're getting healthful exercise, too! (And forget the elevators and escalators—take the stairs.) Take a walk on the beach or to the corner store; just don't buy junk food for the return trip. Ride a bicycle, stroll through your neighborhood, and when the weather doesn't cooperate, "walk the mall."

><
>
> *Everywhere is walking distance if you have the time.*
> —STEVEN WRIGHT, AMERICAN COMEDIAN

Try to incorporate at least one of these exercise suggestions each day.

DAY 137

Don't wait until you smell smoke—learn to read your body's symptoms and discern the familiar warning signs. At the first sign of fire or flames burning where they shouldn't be, stop everything to *rest, fast,* and *exercise* a little.

><
>
> *Conceive it. Believe it. Achieve it.*
> —ANONYMOUS

It doesn't take much to recharge the human battery.

DAY 138

According to medicinal herbalist Dr. James A. Duke, recent research revealed five compounds in mustard that inhibit cancer caused by exposure to tobacco smoke! Mustard applied to skin surfaces causes blood vessels to enlarge and shed body heat, which explains its use for treating congestion in head afflictions, neuralgia, or muscle spasms.[35]

> *Look to your health; and if you have it, praise God, and value it next to a good conscience; for health is the second blessing that we mortals are capable of; a blessing that money cannot buy.*
>
> —IZAAK WALTON, AUTHOR

Inhaled steam produced by hot water poured over bruised mustard seeds is good for colds and headaches.

DAY 139

Turmeric's essential oil has been proven to exhibit anti-inflammatory and antiarthritic qualities. It is a pain reliever older than aspirin that rivals the newest exotic painkillers in its ability to relieve aches and pains without upsetting the stomach.[36]

> *Their father Israel said to them, "If it must be so, then do this: Take some of the best fruits of the land in your vessels and carry down a present for the man—a little balm and a little honey, spices and myrrh, pistachio nuts and almonds."*
>
> —GENESIS 43:11

Instead of reaching for an aspirin to treat your next headache, use turmeric.

DAY 140

Two biblical examples that illustrate the virtually untapped power of music stand out to me. First, when King Saul fell victim to an evil spirit, all it took was David playing his harp to bring deliverance and sweet relief. Second, when the Israelites encircled impregnable Jericho and blew their trumpets and shouted as commanded by God, the walls came tumbling down "without a shot." (See Joshua 6.)

And so it was, whenever the spirit from God was upon Saul, that David would take a harp and play it with his hand. Then Saul would become refreshed and well, and the distressing spirit would depart from him.

—1 SAMUEL 16:23

Music is a gift from God that possesses healing and delivering powers, so we should use this gift wisely.

DAY 141

Most ancient "primitive" people consumed a diet very similar to the diet of the Bible and the original intent of our Creator. Of course, other factors figure in our health picture as well—genetics, environmental toxins, lifestyle choices, emotional and mental factors, and cultural trends that affect health. But diet remains the *single most influential factor in overall human health*. If you eat healthy, you will be healthy!

Whether you eat or drink, or whatever you do, do all to the glory of God.

—1 CORINTHIANS 10:31

Because "you are what you eat," make a conscious effort to eat healthy foods.

DAY 142

Many of us have heard the rationale for the "Genesis Diet" championed by many sincere and intelligent health experts. This diet is based on Genesis 1:29, which gave Adam and Eve instructions to eat liberally from the plant foods lavishly provided in the Garden of Eden.

However, *after* humanity's exodus from the Garden of Eden, the proteins unique to animal foods became increasingly important to a race now dependent on heavy labor, speed, and physical strength to survive. God codified approved animal protein sources as recorded in the Old Testament (Lev. 11; Deut. 14).

For the LORD gives wisdom; from His mouth come wisdom and understanding.

—PROVERBS 2:6

Rediscover the joys of an imaginative journey through reading. Keep a collection of spirit-nourishing books on your bedside table.

DAY 143

Modern society is riddled with myths about primitive people being brutish, savage, and of low intelligence.

Most of us have an image of our ancestors' primitive life-styles that paints them as undernourished, animalistic, filthy, and virtually semi-human people plagued by illness and ignorance. In truth, many of our ancestors experienced robust health—often until death.

Though a high percentage of people in primitive societies died during infancy or while still young, it was largely because our modern technological benefits, for example, of crisis care, and particularly our knowledge about basic sanitation, was unavailable. (Again, the Jewish people of the Bible were the significant exception because of God's ultramodern sanitation guidelines.)

❧

Don't worry about your children, walk at least a mile a day, eat as little processed food as possible.

—DAVID DAVIES, GERONTOLOGIST

Seek out nutritious fermented or sprouted whole-grain bread instead of commercially produced white bread.

DAY 144

In primitive tribes, once married, couples seemed to space their children to permit the mother to maintain her full health and strength and to assure the safety and physical excellence of subsequent offspring. The healthy bodies, homogeneous reproduction, emotional stability, and freedom from degenerative ills enjoyed by such primitive societies contrast sharply from modern individuals existing on the impoverished foods of civilization—sugar, white flour, pasteurized milk, and convenience foods filled with chemical preservatives and additives.

❧

Now therefore, listen to me, my children, for blessed are those who keep my ways.
—PROVERBS 8:32

Avoid eating turkey for lunch. It contains tryptophan, which can cause drowsiness.

DAY 145

We are still discovering ways the brain in your gut mirrors the central nervous system. Nearly every substance that helps run and control the *brain* has turned up in the *gut!* Major neurotransmitters associated with the brain—including serotonin, dopamine, glutamate, norepinephrine, and nitric oxide—are found in plentiful amounts in the gut as well.

The mass of gray matter between your ears is immensely important to your well-being, but you should never discount the vital importance of your "second brain"—the gut.

❧

The brain in the bowel has got to work right, or no one will have the luxury to think at all.
—DR. MICHAEL GERSHON, PROFESSOR,
COLUMBIA PRESBYTERIAN MEDICAL CENTER

Be sure to take in the recommended dose of fiber each day to keep your "gut" operating at its best.

DAY 146

An obscure race of people attempting to cross the Sinai Peninsula about 3,500 years ago received a highly advanced system of disease prevention and medical hygiene. The people followed these instructions and somehow escaped the communicable diseases and social ills that devastated other civilizations over the millennia, just as they were promised.

🍃

If you diligently heed the voice of the LORD your God...I will put none of these diseases on you which I have brought on the Egyptians. For I am the LORD who heals you.

—EXODUS 15:26

Blue-green algae is rich in omega-6 fatty acids, beta-carotene, and trace minerals. Take 2 teaspoons daily to combat fatigue, arthritis, psoriasis, acne, and eczema.

DAY 147

Autoinoculation of the eyes and nose from contaminated fingertips is particularly dangerous because the eyes and nose provide a direct pathway to the upper respiratory tract. (Some diseases enter the body through the mouth, but fluids in the mouth and stomach combat pathogens very effectively.) Upper respiratory problems, including sinus problems, account for eight of every ten visits to doctors' offices. The average adult battles four colds per year (six colds annually for children), and nearly one person in three has allergies.

🍃

Sickness is the vengeance of nature for the violation of her laws.
—CHARLES SIMMONS, CONTEMPORARY AUTHOR

Begin to rid yourself of the habit of constantly touching your eyes, nose, or face with unwashed hands.

DAY 148

These treasure hunters have discovered valuable microbes:

- An employee of Sandoz Pharmaceutical took a vacation in Norway and gathered a soil sample containing a mold that later led to the development of cyclosporine, the celebrated anti-rejection drug used in organ transplants.
- In the soil of an Indonesian temple a scientist discovered microbes that can turn starch into sugar.
- A researcher on a golf course in Japan picked up a clump of soil that produced a drug now used to cure parasitic infections plaguing livestock.[37]

In each case, God led human beings to "discover" the natural elements already present in His world, which could be used to bring healing to the human race.

Behold, I will bring it health and healing; I will heal them and reveal to them the abundance of peace and truth.

—JEREMIAH 33:6

Recognize and thank God for His healing power to perform miracles, as well as the natural remedies He has placed in the earth for our healing.

DAY 149

Our immune systems need regular exposure to naturally occurring soil organisms for long-term health! The immune system of a child deprived of early exposure to soil organisms may seriously overreact when exposed to various benign intruders later in life. It seems to be a consequence of our lost connection with earth that children and adults develop allergies, autoimmune diseases, and certain types of asthma.

For dust you are, and to dust you shall return.
—GENESIS 3:19

As you reconnect with the earth God formed you from and placed you in, your risk potential for disease will greatly decline.

DAY 150

The *beneficial* bacteria in the environment and in your gut serve as your first line of immune defense against the *unfriendly* bacteria and fungi without and within. This is the "doubled-edged sword" of hygiene: to keep your immune system from being overloaded with harmful substances, and still be exposed to the environment enough to "set" and properly program your immune responses for maximum effectiveness.

Take care of your body with steadfast fidelity.
The soul must see through these eyes alone, and
if they are dim, the whole world is clouded.
—JOHANN WOLFGANG VON GOETHE, GERMAN
POET AND PHILOSOPHER

If you are frequently coming down with colds or sinus infections, you may have an immune system that is out of balance. Try taking echinacea tablets, which will naturally enhance the immune system and help prevent colds and the flu.

DAY 151

Although we may understand the three simple steps to health, most of us are careening down a different path, following the "modern prescription for illness." It is an easily accessible path of least resistance—simply follow the standard American diet (SAD), consume whatever you find at America's fast-food restaurants, and fill your homes and bodies with toxic chemicals hidden in common items that advertisements make you believe you can't live without. Unfortunately, the destination is the same for all travelers—illness that is entirely *preventable* by taking the road less traveled.

> *Two roads diverged in a wood, and I—*
> *I took the one less traveled by,*
> *And that has made all the difference.*
> —ROBERT FROST

Commit right now to eliminate all fast food from your diet.

DAY 152

Under ideal conditions, everyone would be born perfect and without flaws. In reality, we *all* carry genetic and metabolic weaknesses and are constantly bombarded and attacked by potentially harmful bacteria, viruses, fungi, and industrial toxins. Because of this, I am so thankful that God has revealed to us how to live above these weaknesses and how to prevent illnesses from attacking our bodies.

> *For I, the LORD your God, am a jealous God, vis-*
> *iting the iniquity of the fathers upon the children*
> *to the third and fourth generations of those who*

hate Me, but showing mercy to thousands, to
those who love Me and keep My commandments.
—Exodus 20:5–6

Make healthy foods readily available in your kitchen—you'll be a lot more likely to choose them over junk food if you've placed them in plain sight.

DAY 153

A top EPA scientific advisor voiced the opinion that "since recent federal government tests have shown that fluoride appears to cause cancers at levels less than ten times the present maximum contamination level, this would ordinarily require that all additions of fluoride to water supplies be suspended and treatment be instituted to remove naturally occurring fluoride."[38] That would be enough warning for me!

Water is the most neglected nutrient in the diet,
but one of the most vital.
—Kelly Barton, Writer

Add a water-purification system to your kitchen tap that will filter out any trace of fluoride in your drinking water.

DAY 154

In general, physicians have little or no training in nutrition. Yet many physicians confidently tell patients that diet has nothing to do with their sickness.

If people would follow genuine biblical nutritional and lifestyle principles, they would largely remove the need for most of the work done in surgical suites and pharmacies! America's surgeons would be reduced to their excellent and vital roles in trauma and emergency medicine due to accidents and other special cases.

꒜

Tell me what you eat, and I will tell you what you are.

—ANTHELME BRILLAT-SAVARIN,
FRENCH FOOD WRITER

Include tomatoes or tomato sauce in your diet at least five times a week—you will significantly reduce the risk of many major diseases.

DAY 155

By my estimate, more than half of the "foods" commonly consumed today were not eaten by our ancestors. Human physiology and biochemistry are geared for the foods the Creator intended for us to eat, not for the high-speed output of modern food "processing" plants or fast-food windows.

꒜

For as the heavens are higher than the earth, so are My ways higher than your ways, and My thoughts than your thoughts.

—ISAIAH 55:9

Eat an orange to glean the health benefits from vitamin C. It will inhibit the process of artery clogging and lower blood pressure. Regular consumption of vitamin C has been found to reduce the risk of heart attack, stroke, and premature death.

DAY 156

Sugar in all of its commercial forms has taken America by storm. Nearly two hundred years ago, the average

American consumed about 10 pounds of sugar per year. Today we gladly push aside healthier fare to gather fully *one-fourth* of our annual calorie intake from sugar—about 170 pounds of sugar each year for each of us![39]

How would you like to see a grocery stock worker drop a pallet of 170 one-pound bags of sugar beside your bed? Would you be willing to sit down and eat a bowl full of sugar (and nothing else) every fourth meal? As bizarre as that may sound, according to the statistics, *most of us are doing just that!*

>

One must ask children and birds how strawberries taste.

—JOHANN WOLFGANG VON GOETHE, GERMAN POET AND PHILOSOPHER

Choose an apple as a healthy snack alternative. Apples have virtually no fat, lots of pectin (a soluble fiber known to lower cholesterol levels), and plenty of vitamin C.

DAY 157

I once heard a man say that the creation of the refrigerator is one of the worst inventions for our health. Before artificial refrigeration, fermentation was the "poor man's refrigeration" to preserve his food in a healthy way. Few Americans from urban or suburban areas know anything about preserving food in this way. Most of the people in the world—including people of Europe, Asia, Africa, South America, and various Third World and emerging nations—still depend on fermentation to preserve foods and to protect them from dangerous organisms in other food and drinks.

🐟

Food, one assumes, provides nourishment; but Americans eat it fully aware that small amounts of poison have been added to improve its appearance and delay its putrefaction.
—JOHN CAGE, TWENTIETH-CENTURY CONCEPTUAL ARTIST

Some of the healthiest Asian foods include legendary pickled preparations of cabbage, turnip, eggplant, cucumber, onion, squash, and carrots.

DAY 158

Three villains inside our bodies cause heart attacks and stroke: *plaque*, which can clog arteries and dangerously restrict blood flow; the *accumulation of platelets* (sticky pieces of blood cells), which clump together and form clots; and the sudden, unexplained *spasms of blood vessels*, which can throw the heart out of kilter. Fortunately, the omega-3 oils can reduce these three risks—or eliminate them entirely!

🐟

Self-reverence, self-knowledge, self-control. These three alone lead life to sovereign power.
—ALFRED, LORD TENNYSON

Eat lots of cold-water fish containing omega-3 oils. These include salmon, sardines, bluefish, herring, lake trout, mackerel, sablefish, whitefish, and bluefin tuna.

DAY 159

Properly prepared meat stocks are extremely nutritious and contain minerals, cartilage, collagen, and electrolytes all in an easily absorbable form. Also, meat, fish, and chicken stocks contain generous amounts of natural gelatin, which aids digestion and helps heal many intestinal disorders, including heartburn, IBS, Crohn's disease, and anemia.

God's miracles can be found in nature itself.
—RONALD REAGAN

Use this kind of chicken stock to help prevent and mitigate infectious diseases.

DAY 160

Although native peoples have always prized the inner organs of game and domestic animals, irrational and unscientific fears about cholesterol have driven organ meats, like liver and heart, out of Western diets. It is true that the liver filters toxins from the body, but the benefits derived from consuming liver from organically raised, grass-fed animals far outweigh any negatives. Liver is one of nature's richest sources of vitamins A, D, B_6, B_{12}, folic acid, iron, glutathione, and various fatty acids.

Beauty of style and harmony and grace and good rhythm depend on simplicity.
—PLATO, GREEK PHILOSOPHER

Organ meats are the most nutrient-dense part of animals.

DAY 161

Spending time over meals with family and friends can be a great stress-reliever. And don't forget that food consumed slowly will digest much better and provide you with the needed nutrition to deal with the rest of the stresses in your life. When eating, don't allow your thoughts to be occupied with worry, irritation, or uncertainty. Focus on your meal and on pleasant thoughts. I recommend conversation with good friends during meals or reading something uplifting, such as God's Word.

There will be time enough to do it all. But not all at once.

—WAYNE SOTILE, AUTHOR

If you usually eat on the run, choose to sit down when you eat—and turn off the television or radio.

DAY 162

Get proper rest. There is simply no substitute for quality sleep. Sleep is so vital to health that I often refer to it as the most important non-nutrient you can get.

A good laugh and a long sleep are the best cures in the doctor's book.

—IRISH PROVERB

Try to get at least seven to eight hours of sleep each night.

DAY 163

Dr. Mark Virkler cited a study comparing two identical farming soils. One was farmed continuously for eight years while the other was allowed to stand fallow or not farmed for one year. The soil from the field that had no Sabbath rest contained 1,097 parts per million (ppm) nutritional solids, while the fallow or rested field soil yielded an astounding 2,871 ppm of nutritional solids! That is almost two-thirds more nutritional solids than the over-farmed soil![40]

> *[Jesus] said to them, "Come aside by yourselves to a deserted place and rest a while."*
>
> —MARK 6:31

Take mini-Sabbaths throughout the day. After several hours of work, take a break to stretch your body and rest your mind.

DAY 164

Elmer Josephson noted that the anti-God government that seized the reins of France after the bloody French Revolution decided to increase the entire nation from a seven-day workweek to a ten-day cycle. Before long, the nation's horses and mules became diseased and died at alarming rates. After scientists investigated, "they found that a return to the seventh day principle was necessary to physical welfare, health, and long life....As someone has said, 'The donkeys taught the atheists a lesson in practical theology.'"[41]

> *On the seventh day God ended His work which He had done, and He rested on the seventh day from all His work which He had done. Then*

*God blessed the seventh day and sanctified it,
because in it He rested from all His work.*
—GENESIS 2:2–3

Don't rush. Allow yourself time to linger. Relaxation and satisfaction have space to grow only when we slow our pace.

DAY 165

Functional fitness is a system of exercise that is truly holistic. Functional fitness utilizes movements that are natural to the body; it enhances the health and strength of every muscle. Unlike traditional bodybuilding, functional training focuses on improving the strength of the body's core (the abdominals and lower back), which also houses many of our most important organs.

There are no shortcuts to any place worth going.
—BEVERLY SILLS, OPERA STAR

Avoid the elevator, and take the stairs whenever you can. It will get your blood pumping, and you'll get in a bit of exercise, too.

DAY 166

Even when you are trying to do everything right, there may be those times when you need some of the Maker's medicine. Fortunately for us, He has supplied them in abundance. In the rigors of daily life, you may need to take a hot/cold shower, anoint yourself with essential oils, and listen to music that soothes the soul. This may seem like a description for a day at the spa—but it's just biblical medicine.

I will sprinkle clean water on you, and you shall be clean.

—EZEKIEL 36:25

To relax, try taking a hot bath with lavender oil mixed in the water.

DAY 167

Originally imported from India and Sri Lanka in Bible times, cinnamon has become one of America's favorite spices. It calms the stomach and may even prevent ulcers. Recent research indicates cinnamon contains benzaldehyde, an antitumor agent, along with antiseptic properties that kill bacteria causing tooth decay and disease-causing fungi and viruses. It may even prevent urinary tract infections.[42]

Nutrition equals life.

—CAROL ANN RINZLER, AUTHOR

Warning: Although the substance is a powerful germicide, do not consume straight cinnamon oil. It may cause vomiting or kidney damage.

DAY 168

The Bible mentions at least thirty-three species of *essential oils* and makes more than one thousand references to their use in maintaining wellness; acquiring healing; enhancing spiritual worship, emotional cleansing, and purification from sin; and setting apart individuals for holy purposes. Why are they missing from our lives today?

Essential oils are highly concentrated essences derived from plants and flowers. Relax with the sedating scents of lavender, lemon balm, chamomile, neroli, ylang ylang, and sage.
—Barbara L. Heller, Psychotherapist and Author

Simmer a small amount of cinnamon oil, cloves, and orange peel in two cups of water on top of the stove. The soothing fragrance will fill your home.

DAY 169

King Saul knew enough to call for the minstrel David when the "blues" set in. You should prepare lists of your favorite music, and then play the music often. See if it doesn't lift your spirits. Certain types of music, particularly what we call classical music and cultural music, can bring about great health benefits.

Worship is like breathing: You were created to do it all the time. It's a lifestyle.
—Joseph Garlington, Minister

A good time to listen to music is during exercise, which can be very inspiring.

DAY 170

Learn to tilt the following stereotypes to lead a happier, healthier life:

- You *should* eat beef, lamb, and other "healthy" red meats.

- You *should* spend time in direct sunlight.
- Make sure you take your children outside to *play in the dirt.*
- You will be healthier if you consume *saturated fat* every day.

While we can't completely go back to the old ways of our primitive ancestors, we can learn from their wisdom in order to *overcome* or *avoid* the modern diseases of civilization. We can make our bodies strong and *more disease-resistant* if we take the necessary steps to do so.

*[The Lord] has given food to those who fear Him;
He will ever be mindful of His covenant.*

—PSALM 111:5

Resolve to let go of any myths you may be holding about your health and diet—and embrace God's wisdom and truth.

DAY 171

Elmer Josephson was a pastor, missionary, and cancer survivor. In his landmark volume *God's Key to Health and Happiness*, he wrote:

> Some ask, why did the Lord make the unclean animals? They were created as scavengers. As a rule they are meat-eating animals that clean up anything that is left dead in the fields, etc. But scavengers were never created for human consumption. The flesh of the swine is said by many authorities to be the prime cause of much of our American ill health, causing blood diseases, weakness of the stomach, liver troubles,

eczema, consumption, tumors, cancer, etc. The
scavengers [are] the garbage containers of the
waters and the seas.[43]

An amazing balance exists in God's creation: the
scavengers are merely God's clean-up crew, but in order
to stay healthy we must avoid these foods as much as
possible.

🐟

*Therefore be very courageous to keep and to
do all that is written in the Book of the Law of
Moses, lest you turn aside from it to the right
hand or to the left.*

—JOSHUA 23:6

Be sure to include protein in your diet that comes from any
of the "cloven-hoofed" animals, including cows, goats, sheep,
oxen, deer, or buffalo.

DAY 172

Your great-great-grandparents probably could not relate
to terms like retirement or nursing home! Most of their
generation lived vigorous lifestyles filled with a lot of
exercise and consumed a diet that was well suited to their
bodies. This combination tended to keep them strong and
healthy well into their eighties and beyond.

Though some people in the ancient past failed to live
long enough to acquire cardiovascular disease or cancer
(two of the major killers in the United States and Europe
today), those who did live long lives rarely acquired these
killer diseases.

🐟

A vigorous five-mile walk will do more good for

an unhappy but otherwise healthy adult than all
the medicine and psychology in the world.
> —PAUL DUDLEY WHITE, AMERICAN
> CARDIOLOGIST

Exercise, combined with the Maker's Diet, can bring you a happy, healthy, and *long* life.

DAY 173

The pioneering research of Dr. Weston A. Price provided solid empirical evidence that the primitive peoples he studied did not suffer from obesity, heart disease, digestive problems, or cancer at the rates we do. Thanks in large part to their primitive diets, these people groups enjoyed levels of vibrant health that have been virtually lost to modern civilization.

✺

> *My son, give me your heart, and let your eyes*
> *observe my ways.*
> —PROVERBS 23:26

Add a few servings of organic eggs, lean poultry, beef, wild game, fish, whole grains, and beans to your weekly menu.

DAY 174

About twenty-four small brain proteins called *neuropeptides* appear in relatively high amounts in the gut, as well as major cells of the immune system. Researchers have even found plentiful amounts of enkephalins—a class of natural opiates in the body—in the gut. The gut is also a rich source of benzodiazepines, psychoactive chemicals that include such popular mood-controlling drugs marketed as Valium and Xanax.

This link between the brain and the gut is helping researchers understand why people act and feel the way they do.

Like Siamese twins, the two brains are interconnected; when one gets upset, the other does, too.
—Sandra Blakeslee, Scientific Writer

Commit to a time of prayer and meditation each day to help calm your mind and your body and reduce the emotional stress in your life.

DAY 175

The leader of the Israelites, Moses, who received the dietary and hygiene system from God, had been trained as a prince of Egypt in the most advanced medical system of his era. Yet Moses did not advocate to Israel the surefire Egyptian prescription for avoiding epidemics. Forensic examinations of mummified Egyptians indicate the upper-class Egyptians didn't receive much benefit from the best that Egyptian physicians had to offer. They suffered from many of the same diseases that afflict us today, especially because they had a taste for unhealthy foods and a blatant disregard for hygiene.

Water, air, and cleanliness are the chief articles in my pharmacopoeia.

—Napoleon

Taking a warm bath every few days is both relaxing and good for you.

DAY 176

As with most instinctive human behavior, autoinoculation (in which cells from the body are reintroduced to the body by touching your eyes and nose with your fingers) also serves an important *positive* purpose. When a baby first touches its fingertips to its eyes and nose, it introduces its immune system to the outside world, triggering the production of key antibodies to protect it from infection and to preserve health. This natural process continues throughout life, keeping the immune system attuned to changes in the outside world.

> *This is the day the LORD has made;*
> *We will rejoice and be glad in it.*
>
> —PSALM 118:24

Add spices such as cardamom, ginger, cinnamon, onions, chili pepper, black pepper, garlic, and hot mustard to your diet to boost your metabolism—and your immune system.

DAY 177

Does the subject of dirt seem boring to you? Did you know that one gram of soil—enough to fill a little packet of sugar—can contain as many as 10,000 species of microbes unknown to science, according to Jo Handelsman, a professor of plant pathology at the University of Wisconsin?[44]

Business Week notes, "Now, for the first time, [Handelsman] and her colleagues…are learning to extract the DNA of these mysterious creatures and clone it. They are finding that the microbes differ so profoundly from known bacteria that they could represent entirely new kingdoms of life—as different from other bacteria as animals are from plants. That means that the proteins produced by these creatures could have properties unlike any other known substances." Handelsman said that several new antibiotics have been identified from such soil microbes.[45]

> When I go into my garden with a spade, and dig a bed, I feel such an exhilaration and health that I discover that I have been defrauding myself all this time in letting others do for me what I should have done with my own hands.
> —RALPH WALDO EMERSON

Reconnect with the earth: make mud pies, plant a garden, get your hands dirty!

DAY 178

A growing body of evidence implies the immune system will never reach its peak defensive capability against foreign organisms and chemical toxins until we reestablish our lost connection to the earth's soil.

Exposure to these microorganisms conditions the human immune system so that it intuitively knows when to produce and activate so-called nondifferentiated T-helper cells (Th cells) that are primarily produced by the thymus gland. These Th cells control the initiation or suppression of the body's immune reactions, and they also regulate many other immune cells.

> Seek the LORD while He may be found,
> Call upon Him while He is near.
> —ISAIAH 55:6

Soy, dairy, wheat, corn, and eggs are the most common food allergens and can cause profound depression and lethargy in some people. If you're allergic to these foods, simply cutting them out of your diet can lift your mood. Give it a try.

DAY 179

Adults and children face even more problems in our toxic world when stress, medications, and poor diet combine to reduce friendly bacteria to such a great extent that unfriendly bacteria begin to thrive. That is exactly what happens when high doses of antibiotics wipe out all the bacteria in your gut.

Once that happens, the race is on to see whether the "good guys" or the "bad guys" are the first to recolonize and set up shop in the empty real estate of the sterile digestive system. Unfortunately, if the harmful bacteria gain the upper hand (as they usually do since they thrive on the typical American sugary, high-carbohydrate diet), poor health soon follows.

All our dreams can come true, if we have the courage to pursue them.

—WALT DISNEY

After a round of antibiotics, you should replenish your "good" bacteria by taking bacterial supplements, available at your local health food store.

DAY 180

When maintaining soil-based organism supplementation, cholesterol levels tend to drop while energy levels increase, and many people notice an enhanced resistance to disease-causing organisms such as colds and the flu. We have even seen improved lymphatic flow and the removal of lymphatic blockages.

He who takes medicine and neglects the care of his diet wastes the skill of his doctors.

—CHINESE PROVERB

Even if you are on SBO supplementation, be sure to avoid contact with persons suffering from colds or the flu.

DAY 181

If we eat unhealthy foods and adopt unwise lifestyles, we may well see our predetermined genetic weaknesses present themselves as devastating symptoms. Unfortunately, many of us exist in a state of subclinical illness (often unawares). That means we can't afford to go through life without taking certain precautions. Fortunately, these precautions are easy to follow—simple changes in lifestyle, diet, and exercise habits—but their rewards are great.

If you need medical advice, let these three things be your physicians: a cheerful mind, relaxation from busyness, and a moderate diet.

—SCHOLA SALERN, ANCIENT MEDICAL SCHOOL
OF THOUGHT

Weigh all the pros and cons before making a decision to receive any vaccinations for your children or yourself.

DAY 182

Essentially, the shortcomings of conventional medicine have spawned countless forms of alternative treatment.

But let me candidly tell you that many of these "alternatives" are as suspect as their conventional counterpart! Care must be taken to ascertain that an alternative approach to health care is scientifically based and fundamentally sound.

‍🍃

It is part of the cure to wish to be cured.
—SENECA, ROMAN PHILOSOPHER

When it comes to vitamins, there is no need to choose time-released ones. The RDA is the amount you need every twenty-four hours. You don't need one-twenty-fourth that amount every hour or one-fourth that amount every six hours.

DAY 183

Our ancestors consumed 30 to 65 percent of their daily calories (and up to 100 grams of fiber a day) from a wide variety of fresh fruits and vegetables. That is why, long before the discovery of vitamins, people who had access to healthy foods lived extremely long lives without vitamin deficiencies or major illnesses. Their protein needs were met by consuming pasture-fed animals, wild game, and fish that were rich in highly beneficial omega-3 fatty acids. These fats protected our ancestors against diseases such as cancer, diabetes, and heart disease—and they can do the same for us, as well.

🍃

Man is what he eats.
—FEUERBACH, GERMAN PHILOSOPHER

Consume at least five servings of fresh fruits and vegetables per day.

DAY 184

Before the advent of mass-manufacturing processes, it was common for long-lived peoples to soak their grains overnight and then allow them to dry in the open air until they were partially germinated or *sprouted*, or to go through an ancient leavening process. From the grains they made bread and other foods.

> *Talk of joy: there may be things better than beef stew and baked potatoes and homemade bread—there may be.*
> —DAVID GRAYSON, AUTHOR AND BIOGRAPHER

Natural carbohydrates you should choose include soaked and fermented lentils, beans, and other legumes. They also include soaked seeds and nuts, fresh fruit and vegetables, and fermented vegetables.

DAY 185

Thousands of years ago, Abraham served his best meat, dairy, and fermented cream curds to entertain his angelic visitors:

> So Abraham hurried into the tent to Sarah. "Quick," he said, "get three seahs of fine flour and knead it and bake some bread."
>
> Then he ran to the herd and selected a choice, tender calf and gave it to a servant, who hurried to prepare it. He then brought some curds and milk and the calf that had been prepared, and set these before them.
> —GENESIS 18:6–8, NIV

Cheese—milk's leap toward immortality.
—CLIFTON FADIMAN, WRITER AND RADIO
PERSONALITY

Eating cottage cheese is a great way to add fermented foods to your diet.

DAY 186

In study after study, cod liver oil has been acknowledged to play a role in the development of the brain, the rods and cones of the retina of the eye, the male reproductive tissue, skin integrity, lubrication of the joints, and the body's inflammatory response.

The strongest principle of growth lies in human choice.
—GEORGE ELIOT, NOVELIST

Choose to add essential oils to your diet by eating fish three to four times each week.

DAY 187

Butter from grass-fed cows, extra-virgin coconut oil, and animal fats have nourished human beings for several thousands of years. However, for the last five decades Americans avoided these fats based on erroneous advice and, instead, increased their consumption of polyunsaturated and hydrogenated fats. As we have mentioned, in direct correlation, the rate of heart disease has increased, as has obesity and many immune system disorders.

✒

If you take your time and keep your wits about you, you can cultivate a wholesome and artful spiritual life that nourishes the whole self—one that will help you enjoy the world and perhaps even save it.

—ELIZABETH LESSER, AUTHOR AND COFOUNDER
OF THE OMEGA INSTITUTE

Choose healthy fats for your diet from whole, grass-fed, cow butter; extra-virgin coconut oil; and properly raised animals.

DAY 188

It is difficult to think of popular modern beverages that qualify as healthy beverages. It is time to return to the lacto-fermented beverages that have supplied beneficial probiotics, enzymes and minerals, rapid hydration, and enhanced digestion to people throughout the world. Some typical fermented beverages include kefir, grape cooler, natural ginger ale, as well as kombucha and kvass.

These lactic-acid-containing drinks help relieve intestinal problems, including constipation, and promote lactation, strengthen the sick, and promote overall well-being and stamina. They are considered superior to plain water in their ability to relieve thirst during physical labor.

✒

Man-made imitation foods are fine for imitation people.

—MAUREEN SALAMAN, NUTRITIONIST

Many scholars believe that the "new wine" consumed in the Bible was a nonalcoholic lacto-fermented beverage.

DAY 189

Unmanaged stress can kill you. It may be the single most important "trigger" of heart attacks. A report in the *Journal of Clinical Basic Cardiology* said that "sudden cardiac deaths" increased significantly during the Northridge earthquake in California in January 1994 and in the Israeli civilian population during the first days of the Gulf War in 1991.[46]

If trying harder doesn't work, try softer.
—LILY TOMLIN, COMEDIENNE

Frequent migraine headaches can be a tip that you have too much stress in your life.

DAY 190

The 58 percent increase in mortality that occurred during the first days of the Gulf War in 1991 was due to an increase in mortality from cardiovascular diseases *on the day* of the first strike on Israel by Scud missiles.[47] Though the Scud missiles launched against Israel in the Gulf War did very little real damage, they were deadly in another way, because people are people, not mere *chemical organisms*.

These effects of fear on the body confirm the very real link between the spirit, soul (mind and emotions), and body. Stress can account for as much as 75 percent of all visits to a physician![48]

Nothing in life is so hard that you can't make it easier by the way you take it.
—ELLEN GLASGOW, AMERICAN NOVELIST

Start lunch with a bowl of soup. Soup sipping encourages slower meals. Studies show that people who begin their meals with soup consume fewer calories during the meal than those who didn't have soup.

DAY 191

Sleep is an absolute and undeniable necessity of life. Lengthy and regular periods of rest are equally important over the long haul. Europeans are far ahead of Americans in this area. By my observation, it is normal for many European families to take extended vacations each year for periods averaging between four and ten weeks! Most Americans struggle just to take a two-week vacation every few years (and many take no vacations at all).

> *Most Americans get only six hours of sleep a night—or less. Insufficient sleep is both physically and psychologically stressful. An extra 45 minutes of sleep can increase your immunity and improve your overall well-being.*
>
> —BARBARA L. HELLER, PSYCHOTHERAPIST AND AUTHOR

At least eight hours of sleep each night is essential for a healthy lifestyle.

DAY 192

Besides giving us the night for regular sleep, the Creator programmed people and animals to rest completely every seventh day. When we tinker with His design, things start to unravel. Even the Creator rested on the seventh day. (By the way, you rest by *stopping* all labor—even the *mental* labor that has been proven to be more exerting to the adrenal system and the entire body than physical labor.)

There remains therefore a rest for the people of God.

—HEBREWS 4:9

Resolve to rest from *all* work—both physical and mental—on the Sabbath.

DAY 193

Functional fitness can be used to achieve great results by people of all walks of life, from the professional athlete who wants to improve performance to the grandmother who wants to climb the stairs to her bedroom more easily. There is no doubt in my mind that functional fitness is the most effective exercise and fitness system available.

Function is a duty or purpose of a thing—or what something is intended for. One of the main things that the body is intended for is to provide structure and movement. Therefore, functional training (fitness) would be any training that enhances the body's structure and/or movement.

—JUAN CARLOS SANTANA, FUNCTIONAL
TRAINING EXPERT

Eating healthy foods is only half of the equation; functional fitness is needed for a truly healthy lifestyle.

DAY 194

God has placed within His creation everything that human beings need to survive—and to thrive. God longs that each and every one of His children should walk in health during his or her life here on earth, and experience even greater abundant life throughout all eternity with Him.

> *Along the bank of the river, on this side and that, will grow all kinds of trees used for food; their leaves will not wither, and their fruit will not fail.... Their fruit will be for food, and their leaves for medicine.*
>
> —EZEKIEL 47:12

Ask the Lord to help you make healthy choices in order to walk in His divine health.

DAY 195

There is research that shows cilantro can aid in the elimination of harmful metals from the body, including mercury, lead, and cadmium. Coriander contains twenty natural chemicals possessing antibacterial properties that help control body odor, and its essential oil treats indigestion.[49]

> *It is with disease of the mind, as with those of the body; we are half dead before we understand our disorder, and half cured when we do.*
>
> —CHARLES CALEB COLTON, AUTHOR

A mild tomato soup prepared with cilantro makes a great wintertime meal.

DAY 196

Historically, essential oils have been inhaled, applied topically, and taken internally. According to David Stewart, PhD, "Seventy percent of the books in the Bible mention essential oils, their uses, and/or the plants from which they are derived."[50] We are constantly learning more about essential oils, but we should consider their immense value when we understand the importance, mentioned so many times in Scripture, given to them by the Creator.

> *The Spirit of the Lord GOD is upon Me, because*
> *the LORD has anointed Me...to give them beauty*
> *for ashes, the oil of joy for mourning.*
>
> —ISAIAH 61:1, 3

Essential oils were not meant to be enjoyed only by people in Bible times; they were also meant for us today.

DAY 197

The Maker's Most Healing Herb #1: Aloes. The aloes of the Bible were used in several forms. Nicodemus evidently blunted or neutralized the bitter smell of the aloes he brought with one hundred pounds of myrrh before wrapping the body of Jesus. Though it may not be the true aloe of the Bible, aloe vera "sailed the ocean blue" with Columbus.

> *Nicodemus...also came, bringing a mixture of*
> *myrrh and aloes, about a hundred pounds.*
>
> —JOHN 19:39

Aloe continues to appear in countless American kitchens and bathrooms as frontline treatment for burns and skin irritations.

DAY 198

The Maker's Most Healing Herb #2: Black cumin (Nigella sativa). This biblical herb, popular in breads and cakes, is used medicinally to purge the body of worms and parasites.

An Arab proverb calls it "the medicine for every disease except death." These seeds taste hot to the tongue and are sometimes mixed with peppercorns in Europe.

> *A man seldom thinks with more earnestness of anything than he does of his dinner.*
> —SAMUEL JOHNSON, ENGLISH WRITER

Include black cumin in your diet, especially if you are suffering from mild digestive complaints.

DAY 199

The Maker's Most Healing Herb #3: Black mustard (Brassica nigra). The Greeks were the first to name this herb. It grew wild along the Sea of Galilee. Its seeds contain both a fixed and an essential oil. It has been used in plasters and has been applied externally to treat numerous conditions such as arthritis and rheumatism.

> *Keep your life so constantly in touch with God that His surprising power can break through at any point. Live in a constant state of expectancy and leave room for God to come as He decides.*
> —OSWALD CHAMBERS, CHRISTIAN WRITER

For arthritis and rheumatism joint pain, apply black mustard directly to the skin.

DAY 200

The Maker's Most Healing Herb #4: Cinnamon (Cinnamomum verum). This delightful herb was part of the holy anointing oil used to anoint the priests and vessels in the tabernacle of Moses (Exod. 30:22–25). It was also mentioned in setting the stage for romance (Prov. 7:17–18). And the ancient Chinese used cinnamon to treat health conditions as early as 2700 B.C.

☙

> I have perfumed my bed with myrrh, aloes, and cinnamon.
>
> —PROVERBS 7:17

Baking dishes with cinnamon is actually good for you—as well as delicious.

DAY 201

The Maker's Most Healing Herb #5: Coriander (Coriandrum sativum). In its green form, this herb, also known as cilantro and Chinese parsley, has been used traditionally as a remedy for acid indigestion, neuralgia, and rheumatism. History records its use as early as 1550 B.C. for culinary and medicinal purposes. It was one of the medicines employed by Hippocrates around 400 B.C.

☙

> God-given, real foods are made for real people. I do not favor processed foods—canned and packaged—because they have lost too many ingredients, and they are embalmed with additives to give them greater shelf life—or shelf death—however you want to look at it.
>
> —MAUREEN SALAMAN, NUTRITIONIST

When placed on an aching tooth, coriander can relieve pain.

DAY 202

The Maker's Most Healing Herb #6: Cumin (Cuminum cyminum). Cumin, which has incredible antioxidant

121

properties, was used in biblical times as a medicine and appetite stimulant. It has also been traditionally used as a remedy for arrhythmia (abnormal heartbeat), asthma, dermatitis, and impotence. The oil of this aromatic seed was used as a disinfectant, perhaps because it is bactericidal and larvicidal, and it possesses anesthetic properties.

> *No matter what your situation, it is your task to set priorities and realistically decide what is possible and what is not possible for yourself. Discipline yourself to focus on what must be done, rather than on your self-doubt.*
> —NATHANIEL BRANDEN, PSYCHOLOGIST

Apply cumin directly to aching joints to relieve pain.

DAY 203

The Maker's Most Healing Herb #7: Dandelion (Taraxacum officinale). One of the candidates for the bitter herbs eaten at Passover, dandelion has been used traditionally as a remedy for cancer, diabetes, hepatitis, osteoporosis, and rheumatism. Contemporary herbalists recommend dandelion almost exclusively as a diuretic for weight loss. (It provides potassium rather than depleting it as diuretic drugs do.) Its leaves are rich in vitamin C and contain more beta-carotene than carrots.[51]

> *Pain adds rest unto pleasure, and teaches the luxury of health.*
> —MARTIN F. TUPPER, ENGLISH HYMNIST AND
> TRANSLATOR

Dandelion roots can act as a diuretic and are useful for treating kidney and liver disorders.

DAY 204

he Maker's Most Healing Herb #8: Dill (Anethum graveo-lens). This common ingredient for modern do-it-your-self "picklers" was so historically valued that the ancient Israelites were required to tithe dill from their supplies. The ancient Greeks and Romans also cultivated dill as a kitchen herb. Research supports dill's three-thousand-year use as a digestive aid.

> *The journey of a thousand miles must begin with a single step.*
>
> —CHINESE PROVERB

Traditionally, dill has been used as a remedy for cancer.

DAY 205

he Maker's Most Healing Herb #9: Henna (Lawsonia iner-mis). This fragrant herb yields a dark red dye popular among Egyptian women and is still used for chemical-free brownish chestnut hair dye formulas today. It was also used in cosmetics and for dying anything and everything that could be dyed. Dr. James A. Duke reports that mummies exhumed after three thousand years in a tomb still had traces of henna dye on their nails![52]

> *The distance is nothing. It's the first step that's important.*
>
> —MARQUISE DuDEFFAND, AUTHOR

Henna contains lawsone, an active antibacterial and fungicide often used to treat fungal infections of the nails.

DAY 206

*T*he Maker's Most Healing Herb #10: Fenugreek (Trigonella foenum-graecum). This herb may be what the Bible calls "leeks." It has long been considered the cure-all treatment for ailments in the Middle East. Dr. James A. Duke reports that fenugreek's bittersweet seeds contain five compounds that appear to help diabetics lower blood sugar.[53]

> *Seeking a healthier lifestyle is an inherently good thing that will help you in many ways in your life. But seeking the perfect body is neither good nor helpful. Seek a healthy body that functions, not a perfect body fit for a display case.*
> —DAVID GIVEN, AUTHOR

Adding leeks to your diet will help your blood sugar levels whether or not you are diabetic.

DAY 207

*T*he Maker's Most Healing Herb #11: Frankincense (Boswellia sacra). Frankincense, one of the three gifts presented to Jesus by the Magi in Matthew 2:10–11, was not native to Israel. This "milk" of the frankincense shrub came from sap seeping through cuts made in the bark of the plant. It was also one of the four exclusive components used to make holy incense for the tabernacle of Moses and is still used by the Roman Catholic Church. It is used in a number of very expensive perfumes and colognes today.[54]

When they had opened their treasures, they presented gifts to Him: gold, frankincense, and myrrh.

—MATTHEW 2:11

Burn frankincense in an incense holder to calm your mind and soothe your senses.

DAY 208

The Maker's Most Healing Herb #12: Garlic (Allium sativum). This ancient herb has more going for it than its unmatched flavor. It is an effective infection fighter, and it even discourages irritating and potentially dangerous mosquitoes and ticks. It is a painkiller, it stimulates the immune system, and it is helpful for treating asthma, diabetes, and high blood pressure.

According to Dr. Rex Russell, "Population studies indicate an inverse relationship between the amount of garlic consumed and the number of cancer deaths in a given population!"[55]

Tomatoes and oregano make it Italian; wine and tarragon make it French. Sour cream makes it Russian; lemon and cinnamon make it Greek. Soy sauce makes it Chinese; garlic makes it good.

—ALICE MAY BROCK, FOOD WRITER

Eating foods with garlic helps to ward off infections.

DAY 209

The Maker's Most Healing Herb #13: Hyssop (*Hyssopus officinalis* or *Origanum syriacum*). This herb, also called marjoram, is harvested in dry places among rocks. A spice, a tonic, and a digestive aid, hyssop was the Bible's "brush of salvation" for spreading the blood of lambs on doorposts to spare the Israelites from the death angel in Egypt.

> *You shall take a bunch of hyssop, dip it in the blood that is in the basin, and strike the lintel and the two doorposts with the blood that is in the basin.*
> —EXODUS 12:22

Hyssop has important cleansing properties, especially in the warding off of disease.

DAY 210

The Maker's Most Healing Herb #14: Juniper (*Juniperus oxycedrus*). This conifer undergrowth still grows in Israel and is likely to be the "algum" timber King Solomon requested of Hiram, king of Tyre, in 2 Chronicles 2:8–9. It yields two forms of cade oil prized for use in men's fragrances, antiseptic soaps, and as a smoked flavor in meats.

> *Send me cedar and cypress and algum logs from Lebanon, for I know that your servants have skill to cut timber in Lebanon; and indeed my servants will be with your servants, to prepare timber for me in abundance, for the temple I am about to build shall be great and wonderful.*
> —2 CHRONICLES 2:8–9

Cade oil is finding new uses as a treatment for human psoriasis, eczema, and other skin and scalp conditions.

DAY 211

The Maker's Most Healing Herb #15: Milk thistle (Silybum marianum). This ancient herb native to Samaria and parts of Israel has been used as a liver remedy for two millennia, perhaps because it contains silymarin, a natural compound that prevents and repairs liver damage and even regenerates damaged liver cells.

The German government has approved milk thistle seeds and extracts for use in treating cirrhosis and chronic liver conditions. It has also been shown to lower blood sugar and insulin levels in diabetics and to help prevent gallstones.

Milk thistle may be grown in home gardens. Its seeds contain eight anti-inflammatory compounds that aid in healing skin conditions and infections.[56]

Here is a little arithmetic to sell you on the tremendous benefits of strength training: One pound of muscle burns twenty to forty calories per day. One pound of fat burns two calories.
—SCOTT REALL, AUTHOR

Grow milk thistle in your home garden, and use it to heal any skin condition you may experience.

DAY 212

The Maker's Most Healing Herb #16: Mint or horsemint (Mentha longifolia). Mint or "sweet-scented plants" are mentioned in two Gospels where Jesus scolded the

Pharisees for gladly giving a tenth of their garden herb harvest to God while failing to honor Him in far more important matters. (See Matthew 23:23; Luke 11:42.) The Jewish people enjoyed mint with their spring Passover feasts and placed mint on the floors of their synagogues. Some species of mint are used to treat Alzheimer's disease and to flavor candies, gum, toothpaste, and liqueurs. They are also used as digestive aids.[57]

> *Woe to you, scribes and Pharisees, hypocrites! For you pay tithe of mint and anise and cumin, and have neglected the weightier matters of the law.*
>
> —MATTHEW 23:23

Peppermint oil is antiallergenic, and you can use it in aromatherapy to stimulate brain activity.

DAY 213

The Maker's Most Healing Herb #17: Myrrh (Cistus inanus or Commiphora erythraea). According to Dr. James A. Duke, there are 135 varieties of myrrh found throughout Africa and Arabia. Myrrh oil was used in the purification of Esther and the other virgin candidates to prepare them to appear before King Xerxes. It was administered both as oils for the exterior and as edible substances for internal cleansing. Persian kings even wore myrrh in their crowns. This expensive, fragrant herb was used to make the holy anointing oil used in the tabernacle of Moses and was one of the gifts given to Jesus Christ by the Magi.

Each young woman's turn came to go in to King Ahasuerus after she had completed twelve months' preparation, according to the regulations for the women, for thus were the days of their preparation apportioned: six months with oil of myrrh, and six months with perfumes and preparations for beautifying women.

—Esther 2:12

If you have been diagnosed with cancer, begin to supplement your diet with myrrh.

DAY 214

The Maker's Most Healing Herb #18: Nettle (Urtica dioica). "Stinging nettles" get their name from the Latin term *urtica* ("to burn") because the tiny hairs on the leaves cause a burning sensation when touched. (The poison is similar to that in bee stings and snakebites.) Mentioned in the Book of Job, nettles may contain substances that alleviate arthritis symptoms.[58]

Carpe diem ["Seize the day"].

—Horace, Roman Philosopher

Consume nettles as a rich source of vitamins A, C, and E, as well as many antioxidants.

DAY 215

The Maker's Most Healing Herb #19: Saffron (Crocus sativus). This flowering herb served as a condiment, sweet perfume, and coloring agent in biblical times. Indeed, it was the world's most expensive spice. One ounce of saffron requires 4,300 flowers.[59] Each autumn, saffron flowers are picked in the morning when they first open because the three orange-scarlet stigmas inside the flowers must be taken before the flowers wilt.[60]

Develop the physical habit of happiness. Depression expresses itself through physical characteristics, such as a sad face and drooping shoulders. Make the conscious effort to stand up straight and smile. Your physiology will produce an uplifted emotional state.

—STEPHANIE TOURLES, SELF-HELP AUTHOR

Just as precious as the saffron was to people in biblical times, so is your health precious to your Creator. Do something today to improve your health.

DAY 216

The Maker's Most Healing Herb #20: Spikenard (Nardostachys grandiflora or jatamansi). A woman of the streets won eternal fame when she humbly anointed Jesus with an alabaster box filled with spikenard, worth a year's wages. The plant was imported from India, and the oils were used in cosmetics and perfumes and medically dispensed as a stimulant.

A woman in the city...began to wash His feet with her tears, and wiped them with the hair of her head; and she kissed His feet and anointed them with the fragrant oil.

—LUKE 7:37–38

Spikenard oil can be used as a muscle relaxant.

DAY 217

The Maker's Most Healing Herb #21: Turmeric (Curcuma longa). This herb and spice possesses tremendous anti-inflammatory and antioxidant properties. Much of the research conducted on turmeric has been done in India, and it shows this herb may be beneficial as a wound treatment, digestive aid, liver protector, and heart tonic. It is a potent spice for cooking and flavor enhancement, and in powdered form it is an antioxidant. It is a reliable chemical indicator that changes color when in contact with alkaline and acid substances.

It is then the truest valor to dare to live.
—Sir Thomas Brown, Nineteenth-century
English Physician and Writer

Use turmeric in cooking to help soothe indigestion.

DAY 218

The ultimate health wisdom available to us is a diet based on health principles clearly described in the Bible, which I have called "the Maker's Diet." It is remarkably well balanced and extremely healthy. Returning to the Maker's Diet as the ultimate primitive diet, based on instructions from the Creator Himself, is certain to contribute to better health for all who choose to do so.

Then God said, "Let the earth bring forth grass, the herb that yields seed, and the fruit tree that yields fruit according to its kind, whose seed is in itself, on the earth"; and it was so.
—Genesis 1:11

Thank God today that He always provides healthy food for His people.

DAY 219

Pork products top the list of favorite foods for many Americans. Pigs did not make the Creator's list of "clean" animals for a very good reason. They never limit their diet to vegetation. They will eat anything they can find—including their own young and sick or dead pigs from the same pen.

With impeccable logic, Elmer Josephson says, "Did anything biologically happen to the swine [since Bible times], or did the digestive tract of man have some kind of miracle transformation? No, the Bible, science and experience have all proven the contrary."[61]

> *Take careful heed to do the commandment and the law which Moses the servant of the LORD commanded you, to love the LORD your God, to walk in all His ways, to keep His commandments.*
>
> —JOSHUA 22:5

Commit today to begin eliminating pork products from your diet.

DAY 220

Heart disease and cancer are still rare among isolated primitive groups in the modern era who eat a more primitive, ancestral diet. One clinical study examined cardiovascular disease incidence and related risk factors among 2,300 "subsistence horticulturists" (people who survive on what they grow, gather, or harvest) on Kitava, a tropical island near Papua New Guinea. The title of the study says it all: "Apparent Absence of Stroke and Ischaemic Heart Disease."[62] What was their secret? The food that they ate: tubers, fruit, fish, and coconut, with virtually no access to Western food or alcohol.

🐟

These all wait for You, that You may give them their food in due season. What You give them they gather in; You open Your hand, they are filled with good.

—PSALM 104:27–28

Select wild fish with fins and scales instead of farm-raised varieties dosed with antibiotics.

DAY 221

Not all primitive diets are alike. Many of the cultures surrounding the Israelites were "primitive," but they were riddled with diseases instigated by their diets and destructive lifestyles. China allegedly possesses one of the oldest continually sustained cultures on earth. Yet many of the cultures represented in modern China eat foods far removed from biblical guidelines.

I can't help but make a mental connection between the virtually continuous streams of Hong Kong flu and Asian flu to our shores from the Far East.[63] God's ways are best— no matter where in the world you travel.

🐟

You can set yourself up to be sick, or you can choose to stay well.

—WAYNE DYER, SELF-HELP ADVOCATE

When traveling overseas, take care when choosing food from street-side vendors, as many of these foods are not only "unclean" according to the Maker's Diet, but also "unclean" from a hygiene perspective.

DAY 222

Sleep disturbances set up vicious cycles of pain, fatigue, and emotional distress that make sleep even more unlikely. Things don't improve much during waking hours, either, for people who do not sleep well. Inadequate sleep increases sensitivity to bowel, skin, and muscle stimuli, thus leading to more pain and distress.

I know from personal experience that when I don't get sufficient sleep, my digestion suffers as a result. On the other hand, a good night's sleep is a great cure for many "gut-wrenching" problems that we face during the day.

He gives His beloved sleep.

—PSALM 127:2

Avoid caffeine in the evening hours to prevent insomnia at bedtime.

DAY 223

The Israelites followed advanced hygienic practices according to the divine instructions given to Moses. And they enjoyed an extraordinary resistance to sickness and disease. God's hygiene system is remarkably up to date. In fact, modern hospitals everywhere follow nearly every one of the original guidelines God laid out in the Bible.

Bacteria can keep us from heaven, or put us there.
—MARTIN H. FISCHER, AUTOMOBILE DESIGNER

Remember to wash your hands before and after preparing meals.

DAY 224

An advanced hygiene system can help to remove the overload of germs from the immune system. This program of advanced hygiene represents the first real advancement in how we wash since the bar of soap was invented about 150 years ago, allowing the body to defend and protect itself against invasion from diseases more effectively. It addresses the proper cleansing of the areas under the fingernails and the membranes around the eyes and nose. These staging areas for germs are virtually neglected by other popular hygiene methods.

Since we have these promises, dear friends, let us purify ourselves from everything that contaminates body and spirit, perfecting holiness out of reverence for God.

—2 Corinthians 7:1, niv

The areas of your body that are most susceptible to germs are your hands, eyes, mouth, ears, and nose. Be vigilant to keep these areas as clean as possible.

DAY 225

Countless numbers of microorganisms live in the soil, in and on plants, and in the human gut. Inside and out we are at one with the earth (or we should be).

Even human intestines—an environment most people consider pretty familiar—are home to perhaps 10,000 kinds of microbes. Indeed, one of the surprises in the decoding of the human genome was that it contains more than 200 genes that come from bacteria. Microbes not only keep us alive; in some small part, we are made of them.[64]

The world God has created is truly amazing!

There is something infinitely healing in the repeated refrains of nature—the assurance that dawn comes after night, and spring after winter.
—RACHEL CARSON, FOUNDER OF THE
CONTEMPORARY ENVIRONMENTAL MOVEMENT

Reconnect with nature today—take a walk and breathe the fresh air.

DAY 226

The soil across the North American continent was exceedingly rich in bacteria and other organisms for thousands of years, and every civilization it supported enjoyed the bounty it produced. After World War II, however, these natural soil organisms were displaced as a result of chemical farming and pesticide usage by commercial agribusiness. Our soil is no longer the same soil God intended it to be.

God made the earth; man made the town.
—WILLIAM COWPER, POET AND HYMNIST

It is much better to buy free-range, organic meat and dairy products rather than the meat and dairy products found in your local grocery store.

DAY 227

The best way to quickly replenish and stabilize friendly bacteria in the gastrointestinal tract and develop a balanced immune system that reacts only as needed is the regular ingestion of live, fermented, probiotic-rich food and supplementation with homeostatic soil organisms. Soil-based organisms (SBOs), in addition to a diet that includes liberal amounts of cultured or fermented foods including yogurt, kefir, and sauerkraut, will create the proper balance your gut needs to be healthy.

Health indeed is a precious thing.
—Robert Burton, Seventeenth-century Author

Be sure to consume cultured or fermented foods on a regular basis.

DAY 228

Soil-based organisms also produce substances called *bacteriocins*, which act as natural antibiotics to kill almost any kind of pathogenic microorganisms and to set up a protective shield in the gut.

Mother Nature offers the best medicine.
—Anonymous

Get back to nature through berry picking. The next time raspberries, blackberries, strawberries, blueberries, or huckleberries are in season, visit a local berry farm and pick and fill your pail!

DAY 229

Most people will never need emergency and trauma medical services for disease-related conditions if they adopt the Maker's Diet and make wise lifestyle choices. Should you develop cancer or some other disease that is not immediately life-threatening, your first order of treatment should be to adopt the principles that would have kept you from disease in the first place.

If you are seeking creative ideas, go out walking. Angels whisper to a man when he goes for a walk.

—RAYMOND INMAN, POET

Make the commitment to continue the Maker's Diet, even during times of health and well-being, in order to prevent diseases in the future.

DAY 230

The word *protein* is derived from the Greek word *proteus*, which literally means "of primary importance." It is translated into Latin as "primaries," that is, the primary constituent of the body.[65] The human body requires twenty-two amino acids to build body organs, muscles, and nerves, and much more.

If you wish to grow thinner, diminish your dinner.

—HENRY SAMBROOKE LEIGH, NINETEENTH-CENTURY BRITISH AUTHOR

Ten to 35 percent of your daily calorie intake should be from protein.

DAY 231

The old harvesting techniques helped preserve and enhance the nutrition value of the grain. After cutting the mature grains in the field, farmers would gather the stalks and loosely bind them upright in sheaves and let them stand overnight in the field before threshing them (removing the grain from the grass stalks) the following day. This allowed the grains to germinate or sprout.

Germination initiates a chemical transformation in the seed grains that naturally neutralizes the enzyme inhibitors the Creator put on the exterior of the seeds. The seeds are activated or come alive, making all of the nutrition within the seed available for digestion.

Man shall not live by bread alone, but by every word that proceeds from the mouth of God.
—MATTHEW 4:4

Choose wholesome whole-grain sourdough and sprouted-grain breads and cereal grains over processed, white bread.

DAY 232

It is said the Chinese fermented cabbage as far back as six thousand years ago. And according to Annelies Schoneck, the Roman emperor Tiberius always took a barrel of sauerkraut (fermented cabbage) with him when he made the long voyages to the Middle East.[66] Fermentation is especially effective in releasing important nutritional compounds through "pre-digestion" that would otherwise pass through the human digestive system, undigested and unused.

*One cannot think well, love well, sleep well, if one
has not dined well.*
—Virginia Woolf, Novelist

Cabbage, both in raw or sauerkraut forms, is an excellent addition to any diet.

DAY 233

God described the Israelites' Promised Land as "a land
of *wheat* and *barley*." Was it coincidence that the young
boy in John 6 brought Jesus five *barley loaves* with which
He fed thousands? Barley has been consumed for thousands of years and is known to improve potency, vigor, and
strength. Roman gladiators at times were called "barley
eaters" because they ate barley before their contests for
bursts of strength. While barley and wheat can be valuable,
their *young sprouts* known as cereal grasses are considered
by some to be true "miracle" foods.

*The Lord your God is bringing you into a good
land, a land of brooks of water, of fountains and
springs, that flow out of valleys and hills; a land
of wheat and barley, of vines and fig trees and
pomegranates, a land of olive oil and honey.*
—Deuteronomy 8:7–8

You can obtain the juice from young wheat and barley grasses
by juicing them yourself or by consuming a green superfood
powder containing the dried cereal grass juices.

DAY 234

The Creator chose to use honey to describe the abundance of the Promised Land, calling it the land of "milk and honey." Honey is one of the most powerful healing foods we have at our disposal. Generations of grandmothers prepared hot honey drinks to soothe sore throats, calm frayed nerves, and ensure a good night's sleep. Asthmatics often swear by honey's ability to help them breathe easier. Honey wipes out bacteria that cause diarrhea. And honey may eliminate such disease-causing bacteria as salmonella, Shigella, *E. coli*, and cholera.

❧

> The LORD [will bring] you into the land of the Canaanites...a land flowing with milk and honey.
>
> —EXODUS 13:5

Honey spread on wheat bread is one of the healthiest snacks you can eat.

DAY 235

Green leafy vegetables are some of the most nutrient-dense foods on the planet, including many nutrients not found in any other foods. Greens contain large amounts of beta-carotene and virtually every mineral and trace element. Many experts believe that ideally we should be consuming between three and five servings of green leafy vegetables per day.

❧

> Refuse to be ill. Never tell people you are ill; never own it to your self. Illness is one of those

things which a man should resist on principle at the outset.
—EDWARD BULWER-LYTTON, VICTORIAN
NOVELIST

If you can't get enough greens from food, try juicing fresh greens or supplementing with a powdered green superfood drink containing dried juices of wheat and barley grass and other vegetables.

DAY 236

If you or someone you love suffers from any medical condition that has been caused by stress, let me reassure you there is hope. As depressing as the facts about stress may appear, you do not have to become a *victim* of stress! Countless numbers of people have overcome the negative effects of stress in the worst possible situations involving stressors beyond their control.

Our reaction to stress is an important key to longer, better living.
—DR. MICHAEL MILLER, MEDICAL CONSULTANT

Change your outlook: try to see the stressors in your life as challenges instead of irritations.

DAY 237

Faith and positive thinking, based on God's Word, are vital keys to recovering and maintaining health. That is why faith the size of a tiny mustard seed can move mountains. When I was sick, I was unhappy; I didn't have tangible joy, *but* I had faith. That was the seed—or foundation—from which my miracle could "grow."

Jesus said... "If you have faith as a mustard seed, you will say to this mountain, 'Move from here to there,' and it will move; and nothing will be impossible for you."

—MATTHEW 17:20

Scripture memorization is an important key to building up your faith. Remember: whatever you put in your mind will come out of your mouth.

DAY 238

One of the first things I learned about personal computers was that many of the seemingly serious problems with a computer can be "fixed" by turning it off! This allows the circuits to reset themselves in the absence of an electrical current. When you "reboot," or turn on the computer again, everything turns up clear and fine in many cases. So it is with the body. Sometimes it is enough just to reboot, to "stop and rest."

Sunday is the golden clasp that binds together the volume of the week.

—HENRY WADSWORTH LONGFELLOW

Do you need to "reboot" this week? If so, spend time resting from your labor and allowing your system the chance to rest.

DAY 239

Other times the situation calls for much more; it requires that you *drop the fork* and rest. This is what the Bible calls *fasting*.

Biblical leaders such as David, Daniel, the prophets, Jesus, and Paul often launched great ministries after extended periods of fasting. Entire nations and cities declared fasts in times of crisis or during times of repentance and soul-searching.

When you fast, do not be like the hypocrites, with a sad countenance. For they disfigure their faces that they may appear to men to be fasting.
—MATTHEW 6:16

Fasting is the Creator's high-powered spiritual tool for receiving a "breakthrough" in body, soul, and spirit.

DAY 240

Even deep-breathing exercises will increase the fat-burning metabolism of your body and "boost your brain" with a rich dose of oxygen. Deep breathing offers benefits that might make a major difference in your health. Your lungs are larger at the bottom than at the top, but most people in America are "top breathers." We live on the shallow breaths common to the sick and the sleeping.

Those who dare and dare greatly are those who achieve.

—ANONYMOUS

To begin a deep-breathing exercise, close your eyes, slowly breathe in from your nose, and then gently exhale through your mouth.

DAY 241

Send someone from our Western civilization for medicine, and they will head for the nearest pharmacy. Send someone from East Asia or Central and South America (who has not been "Westernized") for medicine, and they would more likely head for the nearest herb garden or herbal outgrowth in the wild. They may return with herbs or essential oils extracted from the herbs of the field.

❧

If you've ever done anything successfully, you can do it again. Imagine and feel certain now about the emotions you deserve to have instead of waiting for them to spontaneously appear someday in the far distant future.

—Anthony Robbins, Motivational Speaker

Make the decision to try herbal remedies rather than over-the-counter medications for minor ailments.

DAY 242

Dr. Duke notes regarding the use of cumin, "My research shows that the spice contains three pain-relieving compounds and seven anti-inflammatory properties. If I had carpal tunnel syndrome, I would add lots of cumin to my curried rice and other spicy dishes."[67]

❧

Fill your mind with the thought that God is there. Once your mind is truly filled with that thought, when you experience difficulties, it will be as easy as breathing for you to remember, My heavenly Father knows all about this!

—Oswald Chambers, Christian Writer

When added to curried dishes, cumin brings a delicious flavor, as well as many health benefits.

DAY 243

We *do* know that essential oils have the *highest ORAC* scores of any substance in the world. The oxygen radical absorbance capacity (ORAC) scale measures the antioxidant powers of foods and other substances. Four important biblical essential oils greatly outperform the highest-ranking fruits and vegetables in existence.[68]

You anoint my head with oil.

—PSALM 23:5

One ounce of clove oil has the antioxidant capacity of 450 pounds of carrots, 120 quarts of blueberries, or 48 gallons of beet juice.

DAY 244

There are three types of enzymes: digestive, metabolic, and food enzymes. The three digestive enzymes are proteases (to digest protein), amylases (to digest carbohydrates), and lipases (to digest fat). These enzymes help the body break down food so it can be absorbed in the small intestine. The body itself manufactures metabolic enzymes that direct body functions and digestive enzymes.

Food enzymes are found only in uncooked raw foods. Prolonged heat kills all enzymes, as does cooking, processing, and pasteurization. That is why we should eat raw foods along with our cooked foods. Lacto-fermented foods are especially rich in beneficial digestive enzymes of all types.

Try to eat meats that have been organically raised, and as many raw fruits and vegetables as you can.

DAY 245

Our own technology and advances in knowledge have ambushed us as our technological and marketing skills advanced far quicker than our digestive tracts.

We process food so it will last for *decades* on a store shelf. Countless forms of these bioengineered grains and fruits are offered to unsuspecting consumers in America's largest grocery stores—usually with no notice or explanation.

It may sound good, but think about it. This is the twenty-first century with its incredible technological advancements—yet our bodies are still "genetically wired" to function best on the foods favored by our ancestors.

"For My thoughts are not your thoughts, nor are your ways My ways," says the LORD.

—ISAIAH 55:8

God's ways with regard to the food that we eat are higher than our society's ways.

DAY 246

Regarding scavengers of the sea, we see media warnings about toxic crabs, clams, and oysters on the East Coast each spring or summer. Why? Scientists literally gauge the contaminate levels of our oceans, bays, rivers, and lakes by measuring the mercury and biological toxin levels in the flesh of crabs, clams, oysters, and lobsters. God's Word will be proven true every time.

> *Give ear, O my people, to my law; incline your ears to the words of my mouth.*
>
> —PSALM 78:1

Eat any fish with fins and scales, but avoid fish or water creatures without them.

DAY 247

A number of aboriginal, primitive societies in Australia, Africa, and South America successfully passed into the twentieth century and enjoyed remarkably low rates of cancer, rheumatoid arthritis, obesity, diabetes, osteoporosis, heart disease, and other "modern" conditions—until they switched to modern diets.[69]

> *And it shall be with him, and he shall read it all the days of his life, that he may learn to fear the LORD his God and be careful to observe all the words of this law and these statutes…that he may prolong his days.*
>
> —DEUTERONOMY 17:19–20

For a cool, nutritious, energizing snack, try frozen seedless grapes. To prepare, pluck the grapes off the stems, place them on a cookie sheet with raised edges, and put them in the freezer for an hour. Eat immediately, or store in a freezer bag for later.

DAY 248

Our Creator established our genetic and nutritional requirements long ago. He caused our ancestors to adapt to the types of foods they could gather, and there is no evidence to suggest that modern humans are any different. Despite our technological advancements, our physical bodies are still designed to consume and thrive on the *same foods* in the *same proportions* that our primitive ancestors ate thousands of years ago!

> *And the LORD God formed man of the dust of the ground, and breathed into his nostrils the breath of life; and man became a living being. The LORD God planted a garden eastward in Eden, and there He put the man whom He had formed.*
>
> —GENESIS 2:7–8

Combine 1 cup low-fat yogurt; 1/2 cup ripe fruit; 1/4 cup almonds, raisins, or granola; and 1 teaspoon honey or maple syrup. Blend well for a nutritious on-the-go snack.

DAY 249

Sleep may very well be the single most important ingredient for digestive health. And it is important to get enough sleep at the right time. Some researchers believe that every minute you sleep before midnight is the equivalent of four minutes of sleep after midnight. Restful sleep will do wonders for your digestion and overall health.

I will both lie down in peace, and sleep; for You alone, O LORD, make me dwell in safety.

—PSALM 4:8

A warm bath just before bedtime can help relax you and prepare you for a good night's sleep.

DAY 250

Individuals were to wash their hands, clothing, and utensils with running water, extensive scrubbing, and a mild astringent. The water was treated with ashes—a key component of soap for millennia—and administered with hyssop, which contained the antiseptic thymol (the active ingredient in Listerine mouthwash).[70] In addition, this biblical hygiene system required that hands be washed before meals and at other key times to ensure cleanliness.

Purge me with hyssop, and I shall be clean; wash me, and I shall be whiter than snow.

—PSALM 51:7

Rinse your mouth out well each time you brush your teeth.

DAY 251

Advanced hygiene preserves the balance between the proper function of autoinoculation in building the body's natural defense capabilities and its negative role in promoting infection by mass contamination through the eyes and nose. Careful cleaning under the fingernails and the membranes around the eyes and nose through advanced hygiene techniques reduces stress on the immune system and helps reduce the occurrence of infectious disease and allergies. Once the overload is removed from the immune system, it can devote energy to eliminating other infections that are present in the body, such as lingering bronchitis or sinusitis.

☙

A man's health can be judged by which he takes two at a time: pills or the stairs.

—JOAN WELSH, AUTHOR

Blend 1 tablespoon grapeseed, hazelnut, jojoba, or sweet almond oil with 2 drops each of eucalyptus, peppermint, and rosemary essential oils. Add the oil to your bath while the tap is running for an energizing experience.

DAY 252

Through the centuries, our society has migrated from living with too little hygiene (ignorant of the deadly potential of germs) to an environment that is too clean.

In 1989, Dr. David Strachan, a respected epidemiologist at Britain's London School of Hygiene and Tropical Medicine, launched a tidal wave of debate with a complex theorem of human immunology development and disease control, saying, "We need dirt."

Dr. Strachan proposed that society's growing separation from dirt and germs may well be the cause of weaker immune systems resulting in the growing incidence of a wide range of maladies.[71]

☙

The earth is the LORD's, and all its fullness, the world and those who dwell therein.

—PSALM 24:1

Do something "dirty" once in a while: climb a tree, make mud pies with your children, lie down on the grass in a park—get in contact with the earth.

DAY 253

Years ago, the food we harvested from the field was covered with beneficial microorganisms that "became part of us" when we ate the produce. Today, America's soil is essentially sterile. Pesticides and herbicides are believed to be the "total solution" in the natural world. They kill virtually every microorganism they touch, much as our overuse of medical antibiotics has reduced the human gut to a burned-out minefield, destroying the good guys along with the bad guys. That is why it can be detrimental to your health to purchase food from your local grocery store.

> *The earth shall yield her increase; God, our own God, shall bless us.*
>
> —PSALM 67:6

Look for free-range poultry and beef when shopping for meat products.

DAY 254

Unfortunately, people who are sick or who are recovering from a sickness tend to seek out "comfort food" such as milk shakes, breads, pastas, cookies, and fries. These are the very foods that promote the rapid growth of disease-causing bacteria! This dysbiosis, or bacterial imbalance in the gut, results in abnormal fermentation in the small intestine.[72] Fortunately, there are much better foods you can eat while recuperating that will get you back on your feet much sooner.

⋗

Only the pure of heart can make good soup.
—BENJAMIN FRANKLIN

Just one cup of a hearty lentil soup contains plenty of complex carbohydrates, protein, fiber, vitamins, and minerals—and almost no fat. Many commercial brands are available—choose an organic variety with low sodium.

DAY 255

Hardy soil-based organisms survive the harsh environment of the gut. Unlike traditional probiotics, SBOs seem to be much hardier and are better able to survive the harsh environment of the intestine until they reach the location where they are most needed in the gut.

⋗

The person who walks through nature is in possession of his soul.
—DAVID MCCORD, AMERICAN POET

Take a walk today, barefoot if you can, and experience the earth that God has created.

DAY 256

Critics claim that exposure to the UV rays of the sun cause higher rates of melanoma and other forms of skin cancer. This might be true for a small population segment—those with compromised immune symptoms who don't consume adequate nutrients (especially healthy fats). However, the people who actually get the most exposure to sunlight in different parts of the world exhibit the lowest incidence of skin cancer. The only logical explanation is that exposure to sunlight is not unhealthy.

The sky is the daily bread of the eyes.
—RALPH WALDO EMERSON

Ten to fifteen minutes of unprotected exposure to sunlight several times a week is essential for healthy skin and bones. Sun exposure also energizes your body.

DAY 257

Exposure to sunlight is only unhealthy for us because of the diets we consume. Rex Russell, MD, notes that when sunlight activates the phytochemicals in healthy foods, consumption of those foods not only blocks the harmful effects of UV rays, but they also produce "antiviral, antibacterial, and anticancer components, as well as pest repellents."[73]

The first wealth is health.
—RALPH WALDO EMERSON

During the winter months or on cloudy days, use a sun lamp to gain the benefits that time outdoors in the sun would bring.

DAY 258

I discovered during my battle with a supposedly incurable disease that once you step outside of the relatively *predictable* world of conventional medicine, you find yourself on a very *unpredictable* hamster wheel of unconventional medicine. It is virtually impossible to wade through the hundreds of "miracle diets," pills, potions, and health programs out there—and I do mean "out there." That is why the Maker's Diet is based on more than just theory and speculation—it has its foundation firmly set in the Word of God.

❧

One should eat to live, not live to eat.
—MOLIÉRE, FRENCH PLAYWRIGHT

Be sure to research the background and credentials of any source of "alternative medicine" you might consider following.

DAY 259

Under normal conditions, the healthy human body is able to manufacture all but eight of the twenty-two amino acids from healthy food sources entering the body. These eight *essential* amino acids must come from other sources outside the body. If even *one* of these eight essential amino acids is missing, the body is unable to synthesize the other proteins it needs—no matter how much protein you eat![74]

❧

My favorite animal is steak.
—FRAN LEBOWITZ, AMERICAN WRITER AND
HUMORIST

Eat meat! A strictly vegetarian diet is ultimately unhealthy, because animal protein is our only complete protein source, providing all eight essential amino acids.

DAY 260

Germinated seeds of wheat and barley and the bread made from them were of great importance in biblical times. This living "staff of life" supplied easily digestible, life-giving carbohydrates. However, the people of the Bible didn't wolf down great quantities of carbohydrates, as we do. They actually ate significantly less food than we do today. They didn't consume a "high-carbohydrate" diet—they consumed a lower-carbohydrate diet by today's standards.

Jesus said to them, "I am the bread of life. He who comes to Me shall never hunger, and he who believes in Me shall never thirst."

—JOHN 6:35

Although it was common for people in biblical times to eat only one meal a day at times, today it is preferable to eat smaller meals more frequently throughout the day.

DAY 261

Every long-lived culture in the world has consumed fermented vegetables, dairy, and meat. Aboriginal peoples of Australia buried sweet potatoes in the soil for months before removing and consuming them. The proliferation of lactobacilli and other friendly microorganisms in fermented vegetables enhances their digestibility, increases vitamin levels, and produces helpful enzymes as well as natural antibiotic and anticarcinogenic substances.

Live each season as it passes; breathe the air, drink the drink, taste the fruit, and resign yourself to the influences of each.

—HENRY DAVID THOREAU

Easy, do-it-yourself lacto-fermented dairy products such as yogurt, kefir, cheeses, cottage cheese, and cultured cream (also called *crème fraish*) are exceptionally healthy and nutritious.

DAY 262

The milk consumed in biblical times differed much from the milk we consume today. The milk of the Bible came from cows and goats and was consumed straight from the animal, or it was immediately fermented. These "live" foods provide excellent health benefits in contrast to today's pasteurized, homogenized, often skimmed and "refortified" milk, which is not only less nutritious but also can be potentially harmful and a major cause of allergies and even heart disease.

You shall have enough goats' milk for your food,
for the food of your household.

—PROVERBS 27:27

Drink at least two glasses of milk per day.

DAY 263

The Bible implies a strong influence of butter and honey on brain function. The raw and unheated form of honey preserves its rich storehouse of naturally occurring enzymes and bee pollen. The brain is made of mostly fat (which butter provides), and it runs on glucose (of which honey is an excellent source).

Curds and honey He shall eat, that He may know
to refuse the evil and choose the good.

—ISAIAH 7:15

Always look for high-quality honey produced locally and sold in its raw and unheated form.

DAY 264

Your Creator knows better than anyone does what makes your body function at its peak capacity while remaining free of disease. He designed the bounty of the earth and a wide variety of foods to be the cornerstone of a long and healthy life. The first and most dramatic step anyone can make toward renewed or greater health is to return to the Maker's Diet, which is based on the sound nutrition principles given to us in the Scriptures.

The fate of a nation has often depended on the good or bad digestion of a prime minister.
—VOLTAIRE, FRENCH POET AND POLITICAL ESSAYIST

God wants you to live a long and healthy life on this earth before you begin your eternal life in heaven.

DAY 265

It is a commonly known fact that approximately three out of every ten people will see their symptoms or behavior change significantly simply by being told and then believing they have received a valuable treatment for a physical condition. In fact, researchers *count on this* happening every time they conduct a scientific "double-blind" study. This is called the "placebo effect," and it demonstrates the connection between our minds and our bodies.

> *Happy people are hugely resilient on the whole.
> One thing happy people know is that they don't
> get to be happy all the time. They can appreci-
> ate the moments, the little victories, the small
> miracles and the relationship with one another.*
> —Dr. Dan Baker, Plastic Surgeon

Make every attempt to keep your thoughts focused on the positive aspects of life.

DAY 266

The "placebo effect" is yet another indication pointing
to the power of our thought life over physical conditions. The placebo effect is especially strong with people
who have no "anchor" of absolute truth and faithfulness in
their lives. Personally, I am convinced that if one hundred
healthy people were told by a physician they had incurable
cancer and that they only had six months to live, approximately thirty of them would die—that's how powerful
faith, even in the negative, can be.

> *[We are] bringing every thought into captivity to
> the obedience of Christ.*
> —2 Corinthians 10:5

Dwell on good thoughts, and good things will happen to you.

DAY 267

People in virtually every civilization and culture have an
instinctive understanding of the power of fasting—from
listening to the "voice" of their natural bodies, if from

no other source. Anyone who has been sick understands that in times of sickness, hunger pangs tend to end. Any attempt to bypass those signals and eat often results in violent regurgitation or other discomfort.

> *When He [Jesus] had fasted forty days and forty nights, afterward He was hungry.*
> —MATTHEW 4:2

You may choose a fast that eliminates sugar, caffeine, carbonated soft drinks, junk foods, pasteurized dairy products, commercial breakfast cereals, or pork products.

DAY 268

The average person feels much better and lives healthier by observing a one-day cleansing fast each week. Many health practitioners are returning to the proven wisdom of selected fasting in the treatment of major toxicities (a prominent feature of certain cancer therapies). Some involve "monofasts" where people eat only one food or fast from a particular food group. Sometimes they recommend that people go on a chicken broth fast, which is a modified fast.

> *The best of all medicines are resting and fasting.*
> —BENJAMIN FRANKLIN

Fasting is an excellent way to break free from food addictions or habits and to launch a healthier lifestyle.

DAY 269

Learn to breathe "from the gut." You know you are breathing from the diaphragm if you see your stomach move in and out. If the only thing that moves or expands is your chest, then you are still living on a shallow percentage of the divine potential for deep breathing.

> *Take a "music bath" once or twice a week for a few seasons, and you will find that it is to the soul what the water bath is to the body.*
> —Oliver Wendell Holmes Sr., Physician and Author

As you breathe, check to be sure your belly is expanding as you breathe in and going down as you breathe out.

DAY 270

An herb is defined as a "seed-bearing annual, biennial or perennial that does not develop persistent woody tissue but dies down at the end of a growing season" [unlike a tree for instance] or "a plant or plant part valued for its medicinal, savory or aromatic qualities."[75] Herbs remain an important source of healing and nutritional support, although many in our Western culture don't realize it.

> *Walking is one of the greatest mood-altering activities of life. A nice, brisk thirty-minute walk, the fresh air, releases endorphins which create a feeling of calmness and well-being. To me it's the best antidepressant on God's market.*
> —Scott Reall, Author

The Maker's herbs were humanity's first medical resource.

DAY 271

Dill seed oil inhibits the growth of several bacteria that attach to the digestive tract. As a tea, it soothes stomach and intestines, relieving upper respiratory ailments. Its oil is so strongly antibacterial that it inhibits organisms such as *Bacillus anthracis*. Dill contains various phytochemicals that act as insecticides; enhance estrogen levels; fight infection, bacteria, and insects; and act as a uterine relaxant.[76]

> *No matter what age I work with between the ages of 40 and 90, I have never seen people plateau in their strength training; they keep getting stronger. And once these individuals become strong, they naturally take up a more active lifestyle.*
> —MIRIAM NELSON, RESEARCHER

To soothe an upset stomach, brew a cup of dill tea and sip slowly.

DAY 272

Essential oils are composed of very small molecules that are able to pass through the blood-brain barrier freely or pass through the skin and reach every part of the body in minutes.

> *You love righteousness and hate wickedness; therefore God, Your God, has anointed You with the oil of gladness.*
> —PSALM 45:7

If you place a drop of cinnamon or peppermint oil on the sole of your foot, you may taste it on your tongue in less than sixty seconds.

DAY 273

The Maker's Diet Healing Oil #1: Myrrh (Commiphora myrrha). In days of old, pregnant mothers anointed themselves with myrrh for protection against infectious diseases and to elevate feelings of well-being. It was also used in ancient times for skin conditions, oral hygiene, and embalming. In modern times, myrrh is used to balance the thyroid and endocrine system, support the immune system, heal fungal and viral infections, and to enhance emotional well-being.

> *"Do everything you can, doctor!"* It's a natural inclination to say this, but it is not necessarily a productive one. Getting more treatments or seeing more doctors does not guarantee better health.

> —DAVID GIVEN, AUTHOR

Myrrh may be used as an insect repellent.

DAY 274

The Maker's Diet Healing Oil #2: Frankincense (Boswellia carteri). In biblical times, frankincense was used as holy anointing oil, to enhance meditation, for embalming, and in perfume. Frankincense was used to anoint the newborn sons of kings and priests, which may have been why it was brought to baby Jesus. Today it is used to help maintain normal cellular regeneration, to stimulate the body's immune system, and as an aid for people suffering from cancer, depression, allergies, herpes, bronchitis, and brain damage resulting from head injuries.

The greatest discovery of any generation is that human beings can alter their lives by altering their attitudes.

—ALBERT SCHWEITZER

To cure a headache, place several drops of frankincense oil on a washcloth or handkerchief, place over your face, and lie down in a cool room until the headache is gone.

DAY 275

The Maker's Diet Healing Oil #3: Cedarwood (Cedrus libani). Cedarwood was used traditionally in ritual cleansing after touching a dead body, unclean animals, or anything else considered biblically "unclean," such as the bedding of someone who had died. Cedarwood was also used in the cleansing of leprosy and the cleansing of evil spirits. It has been used by cultures around the world for embalming, medicine, disinfecting, personal hygiene, and skin problems. Today cedarwood is used as an insect repellant and for tuberculosis, bronchitis, gonorrhea, and skin disorders (such as acne or psoriasis). Cedarwood has the highest concentration of sesquiterpenes, which can enhance cellular oxygen.

Let the LORD be magnified, who has pleasure in the prosperity of His servant.

—PSALM 35:27

Cedarwood oil can be used as a hair loss treatment.

DAY 276

The Maker's Diet Healing Oil #4: Cinnamon (Cinnamomum verum). Cinnamon and cassia are actually two species of the genus *Cinnamomum* and have similar fragrances. Both are very effective antibacterial and antiviral agents that God provided to protect the Israelites from disease. They support the human immune system in the battle against influenza and cold viruses. (Do not apply these powerful oils to sensitive areas of the body since they may be slightly caustic and irritating in these areas. If irritation occurs, apply vegetable oil immediately to "cool off" the skin.)

> *Peace be to you, peace to your house, and peace to all that you have!*
>
> —1 SAMUEL 25:6

Apply cinnamon oil to the soles of your feet or inhale the oil to gain its benefits.

DAY 277

The Maker's Diet Healing Oil #5: Cassia (Cinnamomum cassia). Cassia was an ingredient in Moses' holy anointing oil. Cassia, a cousin of cinnamon, is a potent immune system enhancer.

> *All Your garments are scented with myrrh and aloes and cassia, out of the ivory palaces, by which they have made You glad.*
>
> —PSALM 45:8

Add cassia to your healing regimen to minimize your risk of illness during the cold and flu season.

DAY 278

The Maker's Diet Healing Oil #6: Calamus (Acorus calamus). This ancient essential oil is rich in phenylpropanoids and is usually used in combination with other essential oils. It was used in holy anointing oil and incense and for perfumes. It was an aromatic stimulant and a tonic for the digestive system. Today it is used to relax muscles, relieve inflammation, support the respiratory system, and clear kidney congestion after intoxication.[77]

🐟

Every little step gets us closer to where we're going.

—ANONYMOUS

Calamus oil is taken orally, inhaled as incense, or applied topically over the abdomen.

DAY 279

The Maker's Diet Healing Oil #7: Galbanum (Ferula gummosa). Historically, galbanum was used as holy anointing oil, perfume, and in various medicines. Today, galbanum is used to treat acne, asthma, coughs, indigestion, muscle aches and pains, wrinkles, and wounds.

🐟

We feel that older people's reduced muscle size is almost wholly responsible for the gradual reduction of their basal metabolic rate. Metabolism drops 2 percent each decade, starting at twenty.

—BILL EVANS, PHYSICIAN AND RESEARCHER

Galbanum oil can be used to stabilize and balance the emotions.

DAY 280

The Maker's Diet Healing Oil #8: Onycha (Styrax benzoin). This essential oil comes from tree resin and is the most viscous of all essential oils. It has a characteristic vanilla-like fragrance and was used as a perfume, was blended into anointing oils, and was used to heal skin wounds and to comfort, soothe, and uplift. Today it is used to stimulate renal output and treat colic, gas, and constipation. It may help control blood sugar levels. It is also inhaled for sinusitis, bronchitis, colds, coughs, and sore throats. It soothes skin irritations and wounds.[78]

A sound heart is life to the body.
—Proverbs 14:30

Onycha is inhaled, applied topically in wound dressings, and massaged into the skin.

DAY 281

The Maker's Diet Healing Oil #9: Spikenard (Nardostachys jatamansi). In biblical times, spikenard was used as a perfume, medicine, mood enhancer, and preparation for burial. Modern science has shown it to relieve allergies as well as migraines. Spikenard supports the cardiovascular system and calms the emotions.

O Lord…You will restore me and make me live.
—Isaiah 38:16

Inhaling spikenard oil can help suppress feelings of nausea.

DAY 282

The Maker's Diet Healing Oil #10: Hyssop (Hyssopus officinalis). As a principal cleanser in biblical times, hyssop
was used in many purification rituals and to drive away
spirits. Modern science has shown that hyssop can be used
to relieve anxiety, arthritis, asthma, respiratory infections,
parasites, fungal infections, colds, flu, and wound healing.
Hyssop metabolizes fat, increases perspiration, and can aid
the body's detoxification of harmful chemicals.

> *Even the youths shall faint and be weary, and
> the young men shall utterly fall, but those who
> wait on the LORD shall renew their strength;
> they shall mount up with wings like eagles, they
> shall run and not be weary, they shall walk and
> not faint.*
>
> —ISAIAH 40:30–31

Hyssop can provide help to balance emotions.

DAY 283

The Maker's Diet Healing Oil #11: Sandalwood (Santalum
album). Sandalwood was used by the ancients for assis-
tance in meditation as well as in embalming. Sandalwood
contains sesquiterpenes that deprogram misinformation
and carry oxygen at the cellular level. It can be used in
skin care, to enhance sleep quality, to support the female
reproductive and endocrine systems, and to provide relief
in urinary tract infections.

"I will restore health to you and heal you of your wounds," says the Lord.

—Jeremiah 30:17

Sandalwood may be used as an aphrodisiac.

DAY 284

The Maker's Diet Healing Oil #12: Myrtle (Myrtus communis). Myrtle was used in various ceremonies in biblical times that involved purification from ritual uncleanness. Today, myrtle can be used to balance hormones, soothe the respiratory system, battle colds and flu, and treat bronchitis, coughs, and skin conditions (including acne, psoriasis, and blemishes).

He gives power to the weak and to those who have no might He increases strength.

—Isaiah 40:29

Myrtle oil may be used as a treatment for asthma.

DAY 285

The Maker's Diet Healing Oil #13: Cypress (Cupressus sempervirens). Ancient healers used this essential oil to treat arthritis, laryngitis, swollen scar tissue, and cramps. Today cypress is used to support the cardiovascular system. It promotes the production of white blood cells and boosts natural defenses. It is generally massaged along the spine, on armpits and feet, and over the heart and chest.[79]

✘

I treated him, God cured him.
—AMBROISE PARÉ, SIXTEENTH-CENTURY ARMY
PHYSICIAN

Cypress oil may promote emotional well-being in times of loss or stress.

DAY 286

The Maker's Diet Healing Oil #14: Rose of Sharon (Cistus ladanifer). Used historically as a perfume, rose of Sharon is used today as an antiseptic, immune enhancer, and for calming the nerves.

✘

I am the rose of Sharon, and the lily of the valleys.
—SONG OF SOLOMON 2:1

Rose of Sharon may be used to stabilize emotions and moods.

DAY 287

If you feel overwhelmed by the stresses of the day, I recommend that you listen to your favorite *worship music* and join in. In my experience, worship and music are virtually indivisible. Of course, worship cannot be limited to music, but it can certainly play a major role in its expression.

✘

When everything imaginable comes against you, worship God. When things finally go your way, worship God. Nothing else will be as creative as worship, because you are doing more than expressing faith in the sovereign God.
—JOSEPH GARLINGTON, MINISTER

To help ease your stress, keep several of your favorite worship CDs in your car and listen to them on your way to and from work.

DAY 288

One people group stands out among the many primitive cultures studied by anthropologists, health professionals, and nutritional historians. This group of people carefully restricted scavengers (unclean meats) from their diet, consumed foods rich in nutrients, and lived a lifestyle that kept them free from illnesses and plagues throughout history—as promised in Exodus 15:26. That group was the nation of Israel, the chosen people of God.

> *If you diligently heed the voice of the LORD your God and do what is right in His sight, give ear to His commandments and keep all His statutes, I will put none of the diseases on you which I have brought on the Egyptians.*
>
> —EXODUS 15:26

Cultivate an attitude of gratitude for God's prescription for health found in His Word.

DAY 289

God's dietary guidelines contain no refined or processed carbohydrates and only a very small amount of healthy sweeteners. The typical American diet is just the opposite. We stray far from God's design with an array of techno-foods rich in empty calories, filled with refined carbohydrates, and woefully inadequate in nutrition. In contrast, the totally natural Maker's Diet satisfies us with unprocessed foods harvested directly from the Creator's bounty. Countless healing miracles occur naturally as our bodies process and use these foods with great ease.

For I am the LORD who heals you.
—EXODUS 15:26

For an easy, healthy snack, try sunflower seeds. They contain as much as 55 percent readily digestible protein and a generous amount of healthy fat.

DAY 290

Modern civilization has managed to infiltrate the culture of many once-isolated societies. Few of them still consume the primitive, simple diets of their ancestors. American travelers are often surprised to find that canned Western-style food, refined sugar, and white flour products are now consumed nearly everywhere on the planet. As you might expect, this transition from primitive diets to modern diets has brought deadly consequences in the form of "modern" diseases, such as cancer. But you don't have to accept this in your own life—as you remain committed to the Maker's Diet, your chances for acquiring one of these diseases is greatly reduced.

I was astonished to find no cases of cancer. This absence of cancer seemed to be due to the difference in nutrition of the natives compared to the Europeans.[80]

—ALBERT SCHWEITZER

Green tea—this earthy, natural energizer is rich in antioxidants and has only one-fifth the caffeine of black tea, so it won't make you jittery or stain your teeth.

DAY 291

The wisdom in our physiology and biochemistry cry out for a primitive, biblical diet with plentiful amounts of healthy meat, fish, fruit, vegetables, dairy, grains, nuts, and seeds. We have departed so far from the wisdom of our forefathers that fully 55 percent of the American diet is "new food"—not designed by the Creator or eaten by our ancestors.

If we ever hope to be counted among the world's healthiest people, we must leave behind our disease-producing diets and lifestyle and return to our Creator's dietary guidelines, as incorporated in the Maker's Diet.

Your word has given me life.

—Psalm 119:50

Keep plenty of healthy fruit and/or nuts on hand for those cases of the "munchies" that often occur in the late afternoon.

DAY 292

Fortunately, the Creator equipped the human gut with its own ways of coping with pain and stress. The gut produces benzodiazepines, the same pain-alleviating chemicals found in antianxiety drugs such as Valium. It seems the gut is equipped to be your body's anxiety and pain reliever! Evidently, if you take care of your gut, it will take care of you.

🐟

*Be anxious for nothing, but in everything by
prayer and supplication, with thanksgiving, let
your requests be made known to God.*

—PHILIPPIANS 4:6

Journaling about the anxieties and stress that you face can be a
healing activity to do before bedtime.

DAY 293

The Bible also prescribes specific techniques for purifying clothing and key instruments or utensils, along with the safe disposal of human waste, proper burial methods, childbirth procedures, sexual hygiene, feminine hygienic guidelines (for the menses), and more.

Leviticus 13 provides detailed instructions for the diagnosis of the disease called leprosy, with strict guidelines for the purification of fabrics contaminated by the disease. It also called for the quarantine of people with any highly infectious disease.

🐟

*Wash yourselves, make yourselves clean; put
away the evil of your doings from before My
eyes.*

—ISAIAH 1:16

Be sure to wash your hands thoroughly after coming in contact
with any person who shows signs of illness.

DAY 294

Advanced hygiene techniques thoroughly *cleanse* or wash away contaminants, but they do not *sterilize* the fingernail beds and body membranes around the eyes and nasal passages. Sterilization using antimicrobial substances does more harm than good, preventing the immune system from adapting to the outside environment; this is especially important where allergies are concerned.

If I had my way, I'd make health catching and not disease.
—ROBERT INGERSOLL, AMERICAN ORATOR

To increase your energy, shower in water that is approximately your body temperature for two to three minutes, then lower the temperature to very cool for fifteen to thirty seconds. Repeat twice.

DAY 295

Dr. Strachan advanced the "overcleanliness theory" after noticing that children belonging to large families were much less likely to develop asthma, hay fever, or eczema. He theorized that older children coming home dirty with all sorts of resident soil microorganisms were actually protecting their younger brothers and sisters by exposing their immune systems to microbes and causing them to build antibodies. He may be on to something!

God Almighty first planted a garden. And indeed a garden is the purest of human pleasures.
—FRANCIS BACON, SEVENTEENTH-CENTURY ENGLISH PHILOSOPHER AND ESSAYIST

Gardening is a fun and relaxing way to experience the soil of God's earth.

DAY 296

Most people aren't exposed to large enough quantities of microorganisms from our soil, dust, air, water, and foods to achieve optimal health on a daily basis. One exception might be veterinarians who specialize in treating large animals. It is estimated they take in large amounts of microorganisms and animal dung involuntarily (primarily through the lungs) when exposed to large herds of livestock.

One veterinarian in the Midwest spends most of his time tending large herds of livestock—on site in the barns, feeding areas, and fields. His associates noticed he was virtually impervious to the usual strains of *E. coli* and other contaminants in old food and even "chemistry accidents" in the clinic refrigerator. His immune system was like iron, and he very rarely suffered from colds or the usual respiratory complaints, conceivably from his exposure to a wide variety of microorganisms.

We lose our souls if we lose the experience of the soil, the forest, the butterflies, the song of the birds.
—THOMAS BERRY, VICE CHAIRMAN, GOLDMAN, SACHS, AND COMPANY

Allow your children to be exposed to the "natural" environment as much as possible by taking them to a farm or petting zoo.

DAY 297

Fermentation is somewhat desirable in the large intestine because it produces butyrate and other short-chain fatty acids that nourish the cells of the intestinal wall.[81] In the small intestine, however, the growth of yeast, fungi, and/or fermenting pathogenic bacteria may damage the gut lining, cause toxic by-products to be absorbed, and impair the absorption of vital nutrients.[82] Instead of eating junk food and feeding the vicious cycle, you can improve the microbial balance in your gut by consuming the nutrient-rich live foods in the Maker's Diet.

If I'd known I was going to live this long, I'd have taken better care of myself.
—Eubie Blake, Composer, at Age 100

When cooking a whole chicken, be sure to remove fat glands and gizzards from the cavity. If making chicken soup, try to include the chicken feet, if possible, for they are full of nourishment-rich gelatin.

DAY 298

Soil organisms seem to be especially well equipped to establish colonies in the entire digestive system, starting in the esophagus and ending in the colon. They attach themselves to the walls of the digestive tract and burrow behind any putrefaction lining the intestinal walls where they consume or destroy unfriendly microorganisms.

It is good to maintain and cherish the health and life of the body.
—Albert Schweitzer

The lowly dandelion packs a wallop of nutritional benefits. Fresh dandelion leaves are loaded with calcium and vitamins A and C. Awaken a sluggish digestive system by eating the bitter leaves.

DAY 299

Empty promises and flashy marketing campaigns aside, many of these "alternative treatments" are incredibly expensive, and some may actually endanger your health. I know from painful personal experience that people who are desperate to get well or to regain some measure of health may grasp at every straw that offers hope. This is not God's way! He wants you to be well, to walk in health. You don't have to guess about what works when He has set forth clear principles in His Word.

Draw near to God and He will draw near to you.

—JAMES 4:8

If you want to improve the health of your body, turn to the One who created it!

DAY 300

The Bible gives incredible information on health, especially diet. The foods eaten by the Israelites made them the healthiest people on the planet during that time period. But in reading the dietary instructions of the Bible, many health-conscious people seem to ask the same question: How could the Creator claim "fats" are healthy food sources for human beings? Doesn't He know that saturated fats and cholesterol are the main causes of heart disease and cancer?

Contrary to the myth, many saturated fats are actually good for you! The truth may not be easy to believe, but it is still true, nevertheless.

We never repent of having eaten too little.
—THOMAS JEFFERSON

Add saturated fats to your diet to properly utilize essential fatty acids such as the all-important omega-3 fatty acids.

DAY 301

Despite the modern hype and controversy over dairy products, the Bible makes it clear that milk produced by clean animals such as cattle, sheep, and goats is a viable food acceptable for human consumption.

Early and primitive societies understood the incredible value of milk products. Butter and cream in particular provide a treasure trove of vitamins, enzymes, and fats that promote healthy bodies and long life.

One of the very nicest things about life is the way we must regularly stop whatever it is we are doing and devote our attention to eating.
—LUCIANO PAVAROTTI, OPERA STAR

For healthy teeth and bones, drink two to three glasses of milk per day.

DAY 302

When the Creator provided protein, He placed it in close proximity to healthy fats needed for proper assimilation of the protein. He also provided *enzymes* as a type of divine "match" to light the fires of digestion.

Enzymes are specialized proteins that trigger, facilitate, and accelerate chemical reactions, while remaining unchanged in the process. These natural catalysts are found in all *living* organisms, especially raw or uncooked food.

The life which is not examined is not worth living.
—PLATO, GREEK PHILOSOPHER

Because food enzymes are found only in uncooked foods, it is best to eat vegetables raw, if possible.

DAY 303

It was virtually impossible to keep milk fresh in Bible days, so the people "borrowed" the fermentation process used to make wine or sourdough bread and used it to preserve their dairy products. The result was what we know today as yogurt, cheese (soft and hard), and what is sometimes called *curds* in the Bible (called butter or butter curds in some translations).

God is the strength of my heart and my portion forever.

—PSALM 73:26

Choose low-fat yogurt and a piece of fruit as a healthy mid-afternoon snack.

DAY 304

Pomegranate is called the fruit of royalty in the Bible and is one of the richest sources of antioxidants. Pomegranates contain high amounts of ellagic acid, an antioxidant with proven anticancer properties and excellent benefits for female health.

Then they [the spies] came to the Valley of Eshcol, and there cut down a branch with one cluster of grapes; they carried it between two of them on a pole. They also brought some of the pomegranates and figs.

—NUMBERS 13:23

Include pomegranate as part of a fruit-filled breakfast for an extra "boost" in the morning.

DAY 305

God created us in His image (Gen. 1:27), and God is a Spirit (John 4:24). Therefore, we are spirit beings who have *souls* (mind, will, emotions) and who live in physical *bodies*. Our "parts" cannot be divided without skewing or misunderstanding the whole.

God made you a complex, interrelated being, fully integrated and interdependent. Even alternative and holistic health practitioners fall into the same error often made in conventional medicine—they try to fix one *system* or *function* instead of addressing the whole person: spirit, soul, and body.

[Jesus] knew all men...He knew what was in man.

—JOHN 2:24–25

Ask the Lord for healing in every part of your being: spirit, soul, and body.

DAY 306

There is a great distinction between the placebo effect and the power of faith. The placebo effect is based on a person's belief or presumption in a *falsehood*, while faith is based on nothing less than the nature, faithfulness, and absolute *truth* of God and His eternal Word.

In my search for health, I had plenty of opportunities to experience improvement from the placebo effect—I believed in almost every one of the so-called "cures" I tried at the hands of seventy doctors and health practitioners. But the truth is that none of them helped me. It took *faith* in God's Word—and obedience to it—to really trigger a turnaround in my life.

> *"For I know the plans I have for you," declares the* LORD, *"plans to prosper you and not to harm you, plans to give you hope and a future."*
> —JEREMIAH 29:11, NIV

Eat chocolate! Recent studies suggest that chocolate is a great dietary source of magnesium, and it contains antioxidants and heart-healthy compounds. Even if it weren't good for you, a delicious chocolate treat is relaxing.

DAY 307

Doctors McMillen and Stern noted a 1995 Harvard Medical School Conference in which a study was reviewed documenting that weekly churchgoers in Maryland were less likely than people who didn't attend church regularly to die from heart attacks (50 percent), emphysema (56 percent), cirrhosis (74 percent), and suicide

(53 percent). Similar results were found in studies of different population groups at three different medical teaching universities.[83]

><

Let us consider one another in order to stir up love and good works, not forsaking the assembling of ourselves together.

—HEBREWS 10:24–25

Attending church regularly and sharing your life with a community of believers can dramatically improve your resistance to disease.

DAY 308

History has proven that the body can heal itself from many serious conditions by fasting, and today the health-care community is beginning to catch on. Even a partial-day fast can be beneficial. The body heals while it fasts—it undergoes an important regeneration process during our nightly break from activity and eating. That is why our first meal is called *breakfast*—we are *breaking* the *fast* that heals.

><

A Christian worker after only a five-day fast declared, "I feel as though I've got a brand-new stomach!" A digestive weakness he had for years disappeared.

—DR. ARTHUR WALLIS, AUTHOR

I recommend a weekly one-day partial fast from dinner to dinner in my forty-day health program.

DAY 309

The most crucial time of any fast is *at the end* when you begin to reacclimatize your cleansed digestive system to foods once again. Do not gorge yourself on breads, meats, or even large amounts of vegetables. Your stomach literally shrinks during the fasting process. It will stretch out again, but this should happen gradually.

> *When you fast, anoint your head and wash your face, so that you do not appear to men to be fasting, but to your Father who is in the secret place; and your Father who sees in secret will reward you openly.*
> —Matthew 6:17–18

Selected forms of fasting may bring improvement to a number of physical conditions, including arthritis, intestinal problems, obesity, and even diabetes.

DAY 310

Deep breathing literally "massages" and moves the soft internal organs inside your rib cage, allowing your lymph system to rid itself of collected toxins and to collect even more. Only deep breathing allows you to tap the "bonus power" of your lower lungs.

> *He gives to all life, breath, and all things.*
> —Acts 17:25

God has placed the breath of life within you, so learn to use it properly!

DAY 311

A botanist named Dr. David Darom has identified and photographed eighty kinds of plants mentioned in the Bible that are still growing in Israel today![84] And according to Rex Russell, MD, thousands of herbal ingredients have been identified by chemists, and the pharmaceutical industry is constantly searching for more plant ingredients to isolate and mass distribute in purer forms. Dr. Russell went on to say, "25 percent of all drugs still come from herbs."[85]

It is a wearisome illness to preserve one's health by too strict a regimen.
— FRANCIS DE LA ROCHEFOUCAULD, FRENCH AUTHOR AND MORALIST

Fresh herbs and spices are much better health-wise than dried.

DAY 312

H yssop was used in purification ceremonies to cleanse those who came into contact with lepers or corpses. Hyssop stops bleeding (as an astringent) and effectively masks odors; it has also been used as a digestive aid.[86]

Listen closely: The signs of serenity are often more subtle than the symptoms of stress.
—BARBARA L. HELLER, PSYCHOTHERAPIST AND AUTHOR

Use hyssop as a remedy for colds, inflammation, and rheumatism.

DAY 313

Perhaps we should consider that the divine instructions for biblical anointing affected the physical realm far more than we formerly believed. You may enjoy significant health benefits by utilizing essential oils for yourself, your family, and your home.

He also made the holy anointing oil and the pure incense of sweet spices, according to the work of the perfumer.

—Exodus 37:29

Visit your local health food store and learn which essential oils are available to you there.

DAY 314

Is it any wonder that water helps heal us when a large percentage of our bodies are composed of water? Men and women have found refreshment and healing in water since the beginning of human history. The Greeks and Romans built elaborate baths that are still standing, and more recently an American president plagued by polio made a pilgrimage to natural mineral baths in Hot Springs, Arkansas, seeking healing for his aching joints.

Having these promises, beloved, let us cleanse ourselves from all filthiness of the flesh.

—2 Corinthians 7:1

Warm up cold feet with a fifteen-minute bath in hot water. For tired feet, go with a cold footbath.

DAY 315

The Israelites of antiquity followed a diet established by God and were consistently healthier than all of their neighbors. Regardless of your religious preference, any honest student of the Scriptures must admit that the wisdom of the Bible extends far beyond the spiritual issues to encompass every area of life—including dietary, hygienic, and moral guidelines.

As for God, His way is perfect; the word of the LORD is proven.

—PSALM 18:30

Make it your goal to be healthy, not to fit into a certain size of clothing.

DAY 316

Clear-cut hygiene guidelines also accompany the Maker's instructions. Generations of Jewish families followed these instructions and enjoyed remarkable resistance to diseases and plagues, which devastated neighboring people groups with no such guidelines.

For cleanness of body was ever esteemed to proceed from a reverence to God, to society, and to ourselves.
—FRANCIS BACON, SEVENTEENTH-CENTURY ENGLISH PHILOSOPHER AND ESSAYIST

Proper hygiene is important in order to prevent disease. Be sure to wash your hands thoroughly if you are around anyone who is ill.

DAY 317

Ironically, the Australian Aborigines *used* to eat great amounts of *fermented* sweet potatoes (a natural source of probiotics and soluble fiber that literally feeds the "good" bacteria of the gastrointestinal tract). These potatoes are naturally sweet, but when eaten plain or in fermented form, they seem to reduce significantly the risk of blood sugar imbalances![87] Unfortunately, sweet potatoes in any form rarely make it onto our favorite foods list.

Open my eyes, that I may see wondrous things from Your law.

—PSALM 119:18

Try to include some form of sweet potatoes in your diet this week.

DAY 318

Americans seem to accept poor health as a normal consequence of aging, while many experience poor health while still young. Meanwhile, researchers continue to gather evidence affirming the importance of the *gut* to overall health.

More and more health professionals believe there is life and death in the long hollow tube called the "gastrointestinal tract." As Americans, we have neglected gastrointestinal health far too long. Most nations and civilizations seem to understand what we have forgotten long ago regarding the critical role of digestive health—most nations except the United States.

*Fear the LORD and depart from evil. It will be
health to your flesh, and strength to your bones.*
—PROVERBS 3:7–8

Include more soy in your daily diet in the form of tofu, soybeans, and soy milk. Abundant in fiber and complex carbohydrates, they are often touted as today's "miracle food."

DAY 319

If you overeat because you feel anxious, your body may be trying to use the extra food to produce more benzodiazepines. We are not sure whether the gut synthesizes benzodiazepine from chemicals in our foods, from bacterial actions, or from both. We do know that extreme pain appears to put the gut into overdrive in order to send benzodiazepine directly to the brain for immediate pain management. Isn't it amazing that God has built into our bodies our very own mechanism to deal with pain!

I will praise You, for I am fearfully and wonderfully made.
—PSALM 139:14

Learn to deal with stress in your life in healthy ways, such as exercise, prayer and meditation, and talking with friends and family.

DAY 320

Proper hygiene is as essential as diet and exercise to optimum health. You can significantly reduce infections, allergy attacks, and other negative health conditions by cleansing your body of toxins, pollutants, allergens, and disease-causing germs.

The direct relationship between good health and good hygiene has long been established. In fact, the first cure for cancer was based in proper hygiene. In the eighteenth century, London's chimney sweeps had an extraordinarily high rate of scrotal cancer until it was learned that those who regularly washed away the carcinogenic soot on their skin did not contract the disease![88]

> *I'll pour pure water over you and scrub you clean.*
>
> —Ezekiel 36:25, The Message

Try to keep your house as allergen-free as possible by regularly dusting furniture and washing bed linens.

DAY 321

More than 50 million people suffer from allergies, and the suffering continues even though many have visited allergists, taken tests, tried shots, and ingested recommended drugs. Allergies are caused by *mistaken immune system responses* to harmless substances such as pollen, cat hair, or dust mites. These responses produce defensive immune symptoms such as runny noses and watering eyes. But living with allergies is not God's best for you! When you begin to follow advanced hygiene techniques, you may find your allergy symptoms rapidly diminishing.

> *The Lord will take away from you all sickness,*

*and will afflict you with none of the terrible
diseases of Egypt which you have known.*
—DEUTERONOMY 7:15

Try to consume 20 to 30 percent of your daily calories from
the healthy fats found in cream, oily fish, butter, vegetable
oils, eggs, nuts, and seeds.

DAY 322

If Dr. Strachan is right (and a growing number of scientists and medical researchers believe he is), then dirt—or to be more specific, the microbes in earth's soil—may be some of our best friends. A recent report in *New Scientist* said researchers have discovered that microorganisms found in dirt influence maturation of the immune system so that it is either functional or dysfunctional.[89]

The earth is full of the goodness of the LORD.
—PSALM 33:5

Experience God's creation to the fullest: spend as much time out
of doors as you can.

DAY 323

For most of us, our overly sterile environment, which has virtually severed our healthy relationship to the earth, is seriously weakening our immune systems. And the sterility of our foods isn't helping our immune systems either. We have learned to increase "shelf life" by irradiating or chemically treating our produce and prepared foods to kill microorganisms. These modern, high-tech processing methods used by food manufacturers remove and destroy many of the most important life-giving nutrients in our food.

*We are the children of our landscape; it dictates
what we consume and who we become.*
—LAWRENCE DURRELL, ANGLO-IRISH NOVELIST
AND PLAYWRIGHT

Prepare your meals with fresh fruits and vegetables, not canned
or frozen ones.

DAY 324

Individuals who make repeated use of broad-spectrum
antibiotics, oral contraceptives, and steroid medications
may set up conditions for overgrowth of opportunistic
organisms in their bodies that are not controlled by drugs
or that are able to recolonize rapidly once antibiotic treatment has ended, causing more disease symptoms. In this
way, excessive antibiotic treatments become "temporary
bandages" placed over more serious health issues with far-
reaching consequences.

In short, it is easier to treat *symptoms* than to do the
extensive medical sleuthing it takes to get to the root cause
of patients' complaints. Medical science routinely resorts to
antibiotics to deal with recognized symptoms, without assuring
treatment or elimination of the cause of those symptoms.

*Drinking freshly made juices and eating enough
whole foods to provide adequate fiber is a sen-
sible approach to a healthful diet.*
—JAY KORDICH, AUTHOR

The next time you visit the doctor for a minor ailment, ask for
any other alternatives to a round of antibiotics.

DAY 325

Soil-based organisms seem to act aggressively against protozoa, worms, and other parasites within the intestines and related organs and tissues. Scientists from the world's leading research institutions, governmental health agencies, and pharmaceutical firms are scouring the soils of the earth for more soil organisms from which to create their medicines.

Our body is a machine for living. It is organized for that, it is its nature. Let life go on in it, and let it defend itself.

—LEO TOLSTOY

Eat chestnuts for better health! The Iroquois, a North American Indian tribe, used to rely on the fresh nuts of the American chestnut tree as a food of great sustenance. The kernel consists of approximately 7 percent fat and 11 percent protein and contains energy-enhancing minerals such as phosphorus, potassium, magnesium, and sulfur.

DAY 326

Step-by-step programs offering inflated guarantees of success are the most dangerous attractions. Something inside us desperately longs to return to the health and active lifestyles we once enjoyed. There is a tremendous temptation to plug in to any promising program that tells us to simply "follow along."

Be careful about reading health books. You may die of a misprint!

—MARK TWAIN

As in many other areas of life, when it comes to health improvement practices, choose the simplest alternative, for simple is usually best!

DAY 327

Michael DeBakey, the famous heart surgeon, studied 1,700 patients with hardening of the arteries and found *no relationship between the level of cholesterol in the blood and the incidence of atherosclerosis.* The Medical Research Council found that men eating butter (a key biblical fat) ran half the risk of developing heart disease as those eating margarine (a man-made fat that is often indigestible and toxic). A study comparing Yemenite Jews in Israel who ate butter with those consuming margarine and vegetable oils yielded similar results.[90]

There is no love more sincere than the love of food.

—GEORGE BERNARD SHAW

Rather than margarine, choose a low-fat version of "real butter" instead.

DAY 328

Goat's milk in particular is *very* good for human consumption because it is easily digestible. (It digests in only twenty minutes versus three hours for pasteurized cow's milk. It contains less lactose (the type of sugar in milk that many find hard to digest) and is filled with vitamins, enzymes, and protein. Sixty-five percent of the world's population drinks goat's milk.

*Changing our diet should be something we choose
to do, not something we are forced to do. Instead
of dreading it, try saying, "Here's another thing I
get to do to help myself!"*

—Greg Anderson, 2005 Speed TV Driver of
the Year

Look for raw milk cheeses in health food stores, and learn how
to make your own kefir, whole-milk yogurt, and other fermented dairy products.

DAY 329

For many concerned individuals, the solution to nutritional deficiencies was to turn to vitamin and mineral
supplements. Unfortunately, what passes for vitamin and
mineral supplements in grocery stores, pharmacies, and
even "health food" stores often amounts to little more than
isolated or synthetic, lifeless chemicals. Thankfully, there
are many quality supplement products on the market.

*Cooperate with your body and it will cooperate
with you.*

—Maureen Salaman, Nutritionist

Be sure to choose supplements that are organically based rather
than synthetic.

DAY 330

The olive branch has symbolized peace throughout history, and olives and olive oil have been used as powerful
remedies for a wide variety of ills. Olive oil is one of the

most digestible of all fats. A diet rich in olive oil contributes to longevity and reduces the wear and tear of aging on the body tissues, organs, and the brain. It reduces the risk of heart disease and cancer, and it can protect against stomach ulcers.

I was always looking outside myself for strength and confidence, but it comes from within. It is there all the time.
—ANNA FREUD, DAUGHTER OF SIGMUND FREUD

High-quality extra-virgin olive oil should not be used in cooking, as some of the nutrients in olive oil become less effective when heated. Instead, mix it into food once it has cooled.

DAY 331

Grass-fed red meat, poultry, and wild game have nourished humans for thousands of years. Grass-fed beef, buffalo, lamb, goat, and venison are valuable sources of nutrients that protect and enhance the immune and circulatory systems. Free-range pastured chicken, turkey, and duck are good sources of protein, fatty acids, and fat-soluble vitamins. Chicken and turkey contain generous amounts of tryptophan, a natural sedative.

He who does not mind his belly, will hardly mind anything else.
—SAMUEL JOHNSON, ENGLISH WRITER

Properly raised red meats provide an excellent source of complete proteins.

DAY 332

We must emphasize the *whole being*—body, soul, and spirit—and provide the individual with all of the tools needed to maintain or recapture complete health and wholeness.

It is clear from Scripture that in each person, spirit, soul, and body are very closely linked. The early computer term "G-I-G-O" (garbage in, garbage out) may best describe the most crucial "equation" available for the human condition. You and I are not computers, but the formula really does apply to virtually every area of human existence. If I allow "garbage" into my body, mind, or spirit, I can expect to "express" garbage.

> *For as he thinketh in his heart, so is he: Eat and drink, saith he to thee; but his heart is not with thee.*
>
> —PROVERBS 23:7, KJV

If you eat junk food and excessive amounts of sugar and preservatives, and favor the unclean foods the Creator warned us about, then you will almost certainly reap an unpleasant harvest of failed health later in life.

DAY 333

All of the great heroes of the Bible, from Abraham to Hannah (the mother of the prophet Samuel) to John the Beloved, were people of fervent faith and devotion. One after another, they demonstrate the power and peace available through prayer and communion with the Creator of all.

Pray without ceasing.

—1 Thessalonians 5:17

Regular times of prayer—not just when you are sick, but also when you are healthy—can be incredibly beneficial to your health.

DAY 334

People of faith have known the truth regarding power in prayer since time began. Now, even the secular worlds of psychology and medicine are finally catching on. Studies are popping up all the time promoting the power of prayer (or meditation). Hospitals across the land have bolstered their "prayer therapy" for the sick and recovering.

The effective, fervent prayer of a righteous man avails much.

—James 5:16

As you pray, God stands ready to meet your needs.

DAY 335

After a longer fast (seven days or more), gradually work your way back to a regular diet over a period of two to four days, depending on the length and extent of your fast. Consult some of the excellent books on fasting available at bookstores for more detailed information in this area.

Is this not the fast that I have chosen: to loose the bonds of wickedness, to undo the heavy burdens, to let the oppressed go free?

—Isaiah 58:6

Be sure to break longer fasts with broths and nonacidic liquids such as raw vegetable juices, vegetables, fruits, and raw cultured dairy the first day.

DAY 336

God created us to *live, move, work, play, overcome obstacles*, and *win victories* throughout life. He never intended for us to sit around and wait for death.

Some confirmed couch potatoes have confidently justified their lackadaisical approach to life by quoting the passage from the King James Bible, "For bodily exercise profiteth little" (1 Tim. 4:8). They conveniently forget that Timothy probably walked everywhere he went and got more exercise in one day than most people do today in a week.

Physical training is of some *value.*
—1 TIMOTHY 4:8, NIV, EMPHASIS ADDED

Start small: if you are not used to exercise, begin with one thirty-minute walk each day.

DAY 337

Newborn babies *instinctively* deep breathe—watch and learn at the next opportunity. We actually "learn" how to "shallow breathe" and rob ourselves of the breath of life. Singers, stage performers, broadcast announcers, and professional athletes pay great sums to voice coaches and breathing coaches to learn how to breathe, project the voice, and achieve maximum strength through diaphragm breathing (which is what they did *naturally* as babies).

><

Then He [Jesus] arose...said... "Peace, be still."
—MARK 4:39

Learn to recognize the sensations of long, slow, deep breaths as
your Maker intended.

DAY 338

Herbs and spices are incredible sources of antioxidants with antimicrobial and anti-inflammatory properties. According to James Balch, MD, herbs have an important advantage over isolated drugs. The powerful chemicals they contain treat specific health problems while other ingredients in the herbs "balance" those chemicals, making them less toxic while improving their medicinal effectiveness.[91]

><

He who enjoys good health is rich, though he knows it not.
—ITALIAN PROVERB

Green grasses, such as barley, alfalfa, grass, and algae, including spirulina and chlorella, are touted as "superfoods" because they are chock-full of vitamins, minerals, enzymes, and chlorophyll. Available in health food stores in powders, capsules, or tablets that contain either single items or blends of grasses, algae, and herbs, these supplements provide quick energy and the long-lasting benefits of green vegetables.

DAY 339

Dr. Duke reports that researchers recently identified certain lignans in some junipers that could be used in the production of etoposide, a drug used to treat testicular and lung cancers. They also found a potent antiviral compound in junipers that inhibit viruses linked with the flu and herpes.[92]

I fear nothing. I am free.
—NIKOS KAZANTZAKIS, GREEK WRITER

Consume juniper tea as a preventive measure against contracting the flu.

DAY 340

I encourage you to anoint yourself with an essential oil and investigate these claims for yourself. Place a few drops of one of the biblical essential oil blends on your palm, making several clockwise circles with your fingers. Then rub your palms together and cup them over your nose and mouth (but make sure you avoid touching your eyes). Deeply inhale the aromatic vapors, then run your fingers and palms through your hair. It won't make your hair "oily," but it will transform the way you feel.

It shall come to pass in that day that his burden will be taken away from your shoulder, and his yoke from your neck, and the yoke will be destroyed because of the anointing oil.

—ISAIAH 10:27

"Anoint" yourself with oil several times each day.

DAY 341

The most effective way to get your blood flowing and to stimulate circulation is to take a shower and *alternate between hot and cold water* for a minimum period of fifteen minutes (one minute hot followed by one minute cold). You should make the water as hot as you can handle without burning your skin and as cold as you can handle it without pain. Alternate between hot and cold at least seven times during this period. If one area in particular is sore, then make sure the water is hitting that area directly if possible.

A warm, luxuriant bath is the ultimate way to boost your circulation and balance your energy flow. Pour a tall glass of your favorite beverage, close the door, turn the lights down, put on some background music, light a candle and perhaps some incense, and step in. Feel yourself melt into a pool of pleasure.
—STEPHANIE TOURLES, SELF-HELP AUTHOR

For aching or arthritic feet or hands, use two buckets or containers of water, one with hot water and the other with cold. Alternate your feet or hands between the hot bath (sixty seconds) and the cold bath (twenty seconds) for a total of twenty minutes.

DAY 342

Diets and health fads litter the landscape of American culture, but the Maker's original plan for your optimal health and wellness is no fad. The Maker's Diet is at once ancient and new, timely yet timeless. Best of all, *it works!*

Regular exercise, starting with something as easy as a daily walk, benefits not only physical but also mental health. The functioning and effi-

ciency of the brain have been shown to improve with exercise.

—DAVID GIVEN, AUTHOR

Remember that God's Word remains the same—the laws He set forth in Bible days still have significance for us today.

DAY 343

Unlike other diets or health programs, the Maker's Diet is designed to improve the four pillars of health—physical, spiritual, mental, and emotional. God wants us to prosper in every area of our lives—spirit, soul, and body.

Memorizing Scripture is the daily habit of supply the subconscious with God's material to chew on.

—BOB FOSTER, CHRISTIAN WORKER

Daily Bible reading and meditation will strengthen your spirit, just as eating right and exercising will benefit your body.

DAY 344

The Maker's Diet is designed for results, but your success depends significantly on your diligence in following the plan. You may experience moments of discouragement when dealing with a new recipe or when facing a week without your favorite junk food or dessert, but it is well worth it to persevere through those times—your future health depends on it.

Since we are surrounded by so great a cloud of witnesses, let us lay aside every weight, and the

> *sin which so easily ensnares us, and let us run*
> *with endurance the race that is set before us.*
> —HEBREWS 12:1

Ask the Lord to help you persevere through the difficult times as you follow His Word and implement the Maker's Diet into your lifestyle.

DAY 345

The Maker's Diet is designed to attack the three *i's*—insulin, infection, and inflammation. By balancing *insulin*, you can improve your physical, mental, and emotional health, and in turn you balance blood sugar, sharpening concentration and enhancing mood.

> *Bless the LORD, O my soul...who satisfies your*
> *mouth with good things, so that your youth is*
> *renewed like the eagle's.*
> —PSALM 103:1, 5

Keep track of the sweets that you eat or how much sugar is creeping into your diet, and take the necessary steps to cut back in order to better balance your insulin levels.

DAY 346

The second enemy that the Maker's Diet is designed to attack is *infection*. By reducing infection, you can lessen the toxic burden placed on your body through your daily contact with germs.

> *The best and most efficient pharmacy is within*
> *your own system.*
> —ROBERT C. PEALE, AUTHOR

Be sure to wash your hands thoroughly or use organic hand sanitizer when you are in contact with anyone who might be ill.

DAY 347

The third enemy that the Maker's Diet is designed to attack is *inflammation.* By lessening inflammation, you can reduce aches and pains and decrease risk factors for such diseases such as heart disease and cancer.

You don't get ulcers from what you eat. You get them from what's eating you.
—Vicki Baum, Austrian Novelist

Use natural anti-inflammatories first to reduce the amount of inflammation in your body.

DAY 348

By attacking these three *i's,* you can improve your appearance and enhance your energy levels, and you can begin to reverse the process of accelerated aging and live life the way you were meant to live it.

The torch of love is lit in the kitchen.
—Anonymous

Satan would love to keep you "sick and tired," but God wants you to live an abundant life.

DAY 349

When you begin phase one of the Maker's Diet, you avoid consuming certain foods and chemicals to which you were addicted (such as sugar, artificial sweeteners, caffeine, or preservatives). You may experience temporary with-drawal symptoms such as headache, flu-like symptoms, increased carbohydrate cravings, less energy, mood swings, or even temporary changes in bowel habits.

The body is the soul's house. Shouldn't we there-fore take care of our house so that it doesn't fall into ruin?

—PHILO, ROMAN PHILOSOPHER

Be sure to increase your water intake during this time.

DAY 350

Negative side effects during phase one may also occur because of the increased cleansing of toxins from the body. This "detox reaction," as it is sometimes called, is an indication that the program is working. The symptoms are usually short lived.

A man too busy to take care of his health is like a mechanic too busy to take care of his tools.

—SPANISH SAYING

If your body is telling you to rest during this time, it is best to do so.

DAY 351

If you mess up and go off the program for whatever reason, do not beat yourself up! You are only one meal away from success. No one is perfect, and no one has yet followed the Maker's Diet perfectly every single day.

Some succeed because they are destined to; most succeed because they are determined to.
—ANATOLE FRANCE, FRENCH NOVELIST

If you stumble and go off the program, you can start back in again at any time—and the results will be well worth it!

DAY 352

If you are put in a situation where you must eat foods not recommended on a particular phase of the program (and this should be a really good excuse!), it is better to consume all of these "forbidden" foods in a one-hour time period rather than several hours or the entire day. Consuming high-carbohydrate or high-calorie foods within a one-hour time period will minimize the amount of insulin your body can produce or overproduce.

You can have big plans, but it's the small choices that have the greatest power. They draw us toward the future we want to create.
—ROBERT COOPER, LEADERSHIP TRAINER

Following this recommendation will minimize the amount of fat your body will store and will limit the amount of damage that "falling off the wagon" can actually do.

DAY 353

While on the Maker's Diet, be sure to make time for fun! I recommend that at least one day per week should be a fun day. On that day, don't do anything at all that even resembles work. If you can plan your fun day outside, that is even better. Being outside in the sun and breathing fresh air is very healthy.

❧

There's a lot of people in this world who spend so much time watching their health that they haven't the time to enjoy it.
—JOSH BILLINGS, HUMORIST AND LECTURER

On your fun day, take a walk through a park or visit a zoo.

DAY 354

Get out in the sun. It is important to spend time in the sun. Exposure to sunlight can be very beneficial for your health and can aid in the balance of hormones, enhance mood, and help to build strong bones.

❧

Let the morning sun shine on you! Bright natural light early in the day enhances your body's internal rhythms and helps you sleep better at night.
—BARBARA HELLER, PSYCHOTHERAPIST AND AUTHOR

Be sure to wear natural sunscreen when spending long periods of time in direct sunlight. Time in the sun is beneficial to your health; sunburns are not!

DAY 355

Take time to chew your food. Digestion of carbohydrate foods begins in the mouth. When you eat starchy, high-carbohydrate foods, it is of the utmost importance to chew each mouthful of food thirty-five to seventy times. That may seem like quite a chore, but it will benefit you immensely.

>❧

For fast-acting relief, try slowing down.
—LILY TOMLIN, COMEDIENNE

When you slow down to eat your food, taking time to chew each bite thoroughly, you will glean greater health benefits from your meal.

DAY 356

Chewing your food not only aids in digestion, but also the action of chewing can stimulate the body to produce certain chemical hormones that enhance mood as well.

>❧

Success to me is having ten honeydew melons and eating only the top half of each one.
—BARBRA STREISAND

Cut foods into bite-sized pieces before putting them in your mouth—this will allow for easier chewing and better digestion when the food reaches your stomach.

DAY 357

The emotions of fear, anger, or sadness have a great effect on digestion, and may even shut down the process completely. When you are emotionally out of balance, it is better not to eat at all. Have you ever experienced a lack of appetite when you received bad news? That is your body's way of telling you not to eat when you are experiencing trauma of some sort.

Better is a dry morsel with quietness, than a house full of feasting with strife.

—Proverbs 17:1

Don't eat when you're angry, sad, scared, or anxious.

DAY 358

When we eat sugar, our immune system can be depressed for up to six hours. When we are angry, our immune system can also be depressed for up to six hours. So if you decide to eat a doughnut while you're angry, half of your day is ruined!

Nothing erases unpleasant thoughts more effectively than conscious concentration on pleasant ones.

—Hans Selye, Endocrinologist Known as the "Father of Stress"

If you must eat when you are fearful or angry, eat healthful foods that do not contain sugar.

DAY 359

While it is true that the people of the Bible consumed a diet that contained liberal amounts of grain and other carbohydrate foods, they were higher-quality, lesser-processed carbohydrates, therefore much easier to digest. And since they ate smaller quantities of food (some believe as much as six times less food than we do), their typical diet was close to a modern lower-carbohydrate diet.

To lengthen thy life, lessen thy meals.
—BENJAMIN FRANKLIN

The people in biblical times ate as much as *six times* less food than we do today.

DAY 360

The people of the Bible would have eaten extremely healthy diets since their birth, so they weren't hampered by increased insulin sensitivity, endocrine imbalances (including thyroid problems), infection, inflammation, and digestive problems common to people who have been reared with the standard American diet.

What your mind possesses, your body expresses.
—ANONYMOUS

When you stick to the Maker's Diet, you are getting back to the basics, eating a diet that closely resembles the diet of the people of the Bible.

DAY 361

The Maker's Diet begins and ends each day with prayers of thanksgiving, prayers for healing, and prayers of petition. It has been scientifically proven that prayer works. Even if you have never prayed before, God promises His Word will never return void (empty), but it will prosper in the thing for which He sends it. We can trust God's promises.

So shall My word be that goes forth from My mouth; it shall not return to Me void, but it shall

*accomplish what I please, and it shall prosper in
the thing for which I sent it.*

—ISAIAH 55:11

As you pray the Maker's Diet prayers each morning and evening, bring your requests before the Lord, casting all your cares on Him, for He cares for you.

DAY 362

The alignment of Life Purpose to start each day will spell the difference between success and failure. Starting each day with purpose coupled with a regular routine to check-in every ninety minutes throughout the day will be the key to sustaining the Maker's Diet and that will produce the lasting results desired!

*Reappraise the past, reevaluate where you've
been, clarify where you are, and predict or
anticipate where you are headed.*

—TONI CADE BAMBARA, WRITER AND DIRECTOR

Realignment cycles should take place every ninety minutes to realign for a quick two- to five-minute splash of energy and focus.

DAY 363

The Maker's Diet helps you *return* to your optimal health levels by restoring your immune system, balancing blood sugar, and creating healthy eating habits that will, hopefully, last a lifetime.

Remember, you are *not* trying to squeeze yourself into someone's fanciful idea about how everyone should look. But by returning to "the Manufacturer's specifications," your body will naturally return to its ideal weight, shape, and strength levels—all without *dangerous side effects!*

> *Victory is not won in miles but in inches. Win a little now, hold your ground, and later, win a little more.*
>
> —LOUIS L'AMOUR, NOVELIST

As you look into the mirror each day, affirm your body as a creation of God, wholly beautiful just as it is.

DAY 364

If you do venture off the Maker's Diet during phase three, perhaps during the holidays, on a vacation, or another special event such as an extravagant birthday or anniversary celebration, you can always go back to phase one or two for a week or two to get back into the groove.

> *Don't quit before the miracle happens!*
>
> —ANONYMOUS

This option is always available, and you will find it to be a great tool in your journey on the path that leads to health—for life.

DAY 365

I designed each phase of the Maker's Diet to produce noticeable results, but not through dangerous, quick-weight-loss gimmicks that cause you to gain more weight after the program than you lose while going through it. Instead, the Maker's Diet shows you how to continue on the path that leads to health *for life!*

> *To Him who is able to keep you from stumbling, and to present you faultless before the presence of His glory with exceeding joy, to God our Savior, who alone is wise, be glory and majesty, domin- ion and power, both now and forever. Amen.*
>
> —JUDE 24–25

I have done my part—now it's *your* turn to implement the Maker's Diet into your life!

Notes

1. Elmer A. Josephson, *God's Key to Health and Happiness* (Old Tappan, NJ: Fleming H. Revell Company, 1976), 160.

2. Peter Rothschild, MD, PhD, unpublished book entitled *The Art of Health*.

3. Dr. Michael D. Jacobson, *The Word on Health: A Biblical and Medical Overview of How to Care for Your Body and Mind* (Chicago: Moody Press, 2000), 11.

4. *Merriam-Webster's Collegiate Dictionary, tenth edition* (Springfield, MA: Merriam-Webster, Incorporated, 1994), s.v. "gut."

5. *The Surgeon General's Report on Nutrition and Health*, U.S. Dept. of Health and Human Services (Public Health Service), 1988.

6. Ibid.

7. Unpublished literature from Kenneth Seaton, PhD, "Why the Need for Better Hygiene," http://www.advancedhygieneproducts .com/why_the_need_for_better_hygiene.shtml (accessed November 17, 2003).

8. Joseph Mercola, "Don't Let Sleep Pass You By," http://www .mercola.com/nograindiet/bottomline/sleep.htm (accessed November 18, 2003).

9. *Lancet* 354 (October 23, 1999): 1435–1439, as referenced in Joseph Mercola, "Too Little Sleep May Accelerate Aging," http://www .mercola.com/1999/archive/sleep_and_aging.htm (accessed November 18, 2003).

10. Josephson, *God's Key to Health and Happiness*, 197.

11. Brian Bretsch, "Winter Brings Cold and Dry Itchy Skin," Barnes Jewish Holiday, http://www.barnesjewish.org/groups/default .asp?NavID+1014 (accessed January 5, 2004).

12. Rex Russell, MD, *What the Bible Says About Healthy Living* (Ventura, CA: Regal Books, 1996), 68.

13. "New Changes for Airline Medical Safety," April 20, 2002, http://www.mercola.com/2002/apr/20/airline_safety.htm.

14. "More Drug Company Conflict of Interest," April 2, 2003, http://www.mercola.com/2003/apr/2/drug_companies.htm.

15. "Wearing Contacts Overnight Boosts Infection Risk," http:// www.mercola.com/1999/archive/contacts_overnight_increase_

infection.htm.

16. Barbara Starfield, "Is US Health Really the Best in the World?" *Journal of the American Medical Association* 284 (July 26, 2000): 483–485.

17. Kevin Lehman, *Keeping Your Family Together When the World Is Falling Apart* (New York: Delacorte Press, Bantam Doubleday Dell Publishing Group, Inc., 1992), 273, citing David Elkind, *The Hurried Child*, rev. ed. (Reading, MA: Addison-Wesley, 1988), 42.

18. Don Colbert, MD, *What You Don't Know May Be Killing You!* (Lake Mary, FL: Siloam, 2000), 92.

19. For details information about the benefits and methods to instill deep breathing patterns, see Davis, Eshelman, and McKay, *The Relaxation and Stress Reduction Notebook*, 2nd ed. (New Harbringer Publications, 1982).

20. James A. Duke, PhD, *Herbs of the Bible: 2000 Years of Plant Medicine* (Loveland, CO: Interweave Press, 1999), 8.

21. Russell, *What the Bible Says About Healthy Living*, 170–172.

22. Gannet News Service, "Discovery Finds Myrrh Kills Cancer," *Des Moines Register DM*, December 17, 2001.

23. "Consumer Research on Dietary Supplements," U.S. Food and Drug Administration, Center for Food Safety and Applied Nutrition, Consumer Studies Branch, http://vm.cfsan.fda.gov/~lrd/ab-suppl .html (accessed November 24, 2003).

24. Jacobson, *The Word on Health*, 166.

25. "Laughter 'Protects the Heart,'" BBC News Online: Health, Wednesday, 15 November 2000, 16:23 GMT, http://news.bbc.co.uk/1/ low/health/1024713.stm (accessed June 13, 2003).

26. Morton Walker, DPM, "Jumping for Health," *Townsend Letter for Doctors* (n.d.).

27. Duke, *Herbs of the Bible: 2000 Years of Plant Medicine*, 203–205.

28. Paul Chek, "The Power of Waiting," C.H.E.K. Institute, http://www.chekinstitute.com/articles.cfm?select=38 (accessed June 14, 2003).

29. Mark and Patti Virkler, *Eden's Health Plan—Go Natural!* (Shippensburg, PA: Destiny Image Publishers, 1994), 132, citing "Exercise: A Little Helps a Lot," *Consumer Reports on Health*, August 1994, 89.

30. Duke, *Herbs of the Bible: 2000 Years of Plant Medicine*, 47–49.

31. Ibid., 210–212.

32. Russell, *What the Bible Says About Healthy Living*, 68.

33. P. Raeburn, "Down in the Dirt, Wonders Beckon: Soil and Sea Yield Unknown Lodes of Useful Microbes," *Business Week*, December 3, 2001.

34. Jacobson, *The Word on Health*, 190, citing Research Update, Institute of HeartMath (Boulder Creek, CO: Institute of HeartMath, 1995).

35. Duke, *Herbs of the Bible: 2000 Years of Plant Medicine*, 54–55.

36. Ibid., 218–220.

37. "Dirt and Health," *Healthy Living*, volume 5, number 10, http://www.primaldefense.ca/securestore/c155120.2.html (accessed June 26, 2006).

38. David Steinman, *Diet for a Poisoned Planet: How to Choose Safe Foods for You and Your Family* (New York: Harmony Books, a division of Crown Publishers, 1990), 225–226.

39. Sally Fallon with Mary G. Enig, PhD, *Nourishing Traditions: The Cookbook That Challenges Politically Correct Nutrition and the Diet Dictotrats*, second ed. (Washington DC: New Trends Publishing, Inc., 1999), 26.

40. Virkler, *Eden's Health Plan—Go Natural!*, 176–181.

41. Josephson, *God's Key to Health and Happiness*, 163.

42. Duke, *Herbs of the Bible: 2000 Years of Plant Medicine*, 77–80.

43. Josephson, *God's Key to Health and Happiness*, 47.

44. Raeburn, "Down in the Dirt, Wonders Beckon: Soil and Sea Yield Unknown Lodes of Useful Microbes."

45. Ibid.

46. J. Muller-Nordhorn and S. N. Willich, "Triggering of Acute Coronary Syndromes," *Journal of Clinical Basic Cardiology* 3 (2000): 73, citing J. Leor, et al., "Sudden Cardiac Deaths Triggered by an Earthquake," *New England Journal of Medicine* 334 (1996): 413–419; S. R. Meisel, et al., "Effect of Iraqi Missile War on Incidence of Acute Myocardial Infarction and Sudden Death in Israeli Civilians," *Lancet* 338 (1991): 660–661; J. D. Kark, et al., "Iraqi Missile Attacks on Israel: The Association of Mortality with a Life-Threatening Stressor,"

Journal of the American Medical Association 273 (19 April 1995): 1208–1210.

47. Ibid.

48. Jacobson, *The Word on Health*, 161.

49. Duke, *Herbs of the Bible: 2000 Years of Plant Medicine*, 85–87.

50. David Stewart, PhD, *Healing Oils of the Bible* (Marble Hill, CO: Center for Aromatherapy Research & Education, 2002), xvi–xix, 96–113.

51. Duke, *Herbs of the Bible: 2000 Years of Plant Medicine*, 97–99.

52. Ibid., 144–146.

53. Ibid., 119–121.

54. Ibid., 132.

55. Russell, *What the Bible Says About Healthy Living*, 198.

56. Ibid., 163–165.

57. Ibid., 149–151.

58. Duke, *Herbs of the Bible: 2000 Years of Plant Medicine*, 179.

59. Ibid., 203.

60. Rut F. Rosevear, *Nutrition in Biblical Times* (Cincinnati, OH: Clifton Hills Press, Inc., 2000), 49, citing Diane Ward, *Smithsonian*, August 1988, 106–107.

61. Josephson, *God's Key to Health and Happiness*, 40.

62. S. Lindeberg and B. Lundh, "Apparent Absence of Stroke and Ischaemic Heart Disease in a Traditional Melanesian Island: A Clinical Study of Kitava," *J Intern Med* 233 (1993): 269–275.

63. Michael Browning, "China's Taste for Critters May Have Aided SARS," *Palm Beach Post*, May 25, 2003.

64. Raeburn, "Down in the Dirt, Wonders Beckon: Soil and Sea Yield Unknown Lodes of Useful Microbes."

65. Protein and Amino Acids, Origin of the Word "Protein," National Academy Press, http://books.nap.edu/books/0309063469/html/109.html (accessed August 19, 2003).

66. Annelies Schoneck from *Des Crudites Toute L'Annee,* as cited in Fallon, *Nourishing Traditions*, 93.

67. Duke, *Herbs of the Bible: 2000 Years of Plant Medicine*, 93–95.

68. Stewart, *Healing Oils of the Bible*, 18.

69. M. Murray and J. Pizzorno, *Encyclopedia of Natural Medicine* (Rocklin, CA: Prima Publishing, 1998).

70. S. I. McMillen, MD, and David E. Stern, MD, *None of These*

Diseases (Grand Rapids, MI: Fleming H. Revell, 2000), 25.

71. M. Downey, "Let Them Eat Dirt," *Toronto Star,* January 10, 1999, F1.

72. C. Pignata, et al., "Jejunal Bacterial Overgrowth and Intestinal Permeability in Children with Immunodeficiency Syndromes," *Gut* 31 (1990): 879–882.

73. Russell, *What the Bible Says About Healthy Living,* 241.

74. Fallon, *Nourishing Traditions,* 23, citing Joseph D. Beasly, MD, and Jerry J. Swift, MA, *The Kellogg Report* (Annandale-on-Hudson, NY: The Institute of Health Policy and Practice, 1989), 144–145.

75. *Merriam-Webster's Collegiate Dictionary,* s.v. "herb."

76. Duke, *Herbs of the Bible: 2000 Years of Plant Medicine,* 109–111.

77. Stewart, *Healing Oils of the Bible,* 287.

78. Ibid., 297.

79. Ibid., 291.

80. Albert Schweitzer, in his Preface to A. Berglas, *Cancer: Cause and Cure,* as quoted in James South, MA, "Laetrile—the Answer to Cancer," IAS Bulletin, http://www.antiaging-systems.com/extract/laetril.htm (accessed November 17, 2003).

81. A. Csordas, *Toxicology of Butyrate and Short-chain Fatty Acids in Role of Gut Bacteria in Human Toxicology and Pharmacology,* M. Hill, ed. (Bristol: Taylor & Francis, Inc., 1995), 286.

82. A. Hunnisett, et al., "Gut Fermentation (or the 'Autobrewery') Syndrome: A New Clinical Test with Initial Observations and Discussion of Clinical and Biochemical Implications," *J Nut Med* 1 (1990): 33–38.

83. McMillen and Stern, *None of These Diseases,* 200.

84. Russell, *What the Bible Says About Healthy Living,* 198.

85. Ibid., 201–202.

86. Ibid., 152.

87. K. O'Dea, "Traditional Diet and Food Preferences of Australian Aboriginal Hunter-Gatherers," *Philosophical Transactions of the Royal Society of London, Series B* 33 (1984): 596–603.

88. Unpublished literature from Kenneth Seaton, PhD, "Why the Need for Better Hygiene," http://www.advancedhygieneproducts.com/why_the_need_for_better_hygiene.html (accessed November 17, 2003).

89. Downey, "Let Them Eat Dirt."

90. Fallon, *Nourishing Traditions*, 26.

91. Russell, *What the Bible Says About Healthy Living*, 202, citing James R. Balch, MD, and A. Phyllis Balch, CNC, *Prescription for Nutritional Healing* (Garden City, NY: Avery Publishing, 1990), 46.

92. Russell, *What the Bible Says About Healthy Living*, 154–155.